ANIMALS IN GREEK AND ROMAN THOUGHT: A SOURCEBOOK

Although reasoned discourse on human–animal relations is often considered a late twentieth-century phenomenon, ethical debate over animals and how humans should treat them can be traced back to the philosophers and literati of the classical world. From Stoic assertions that humans owe nothing to animals that are intellectually foreign to them, to Plutarch's impassioned arguments for animals as sentient and rational beings, it is clear that modern debate owes much to Greco-Roman thought.

Animals in Greek and Roman Thought brings together new translations of classical passages which contributed to ancient debate on the nature of animals and their relationship to human beings. The selections chosen come primarily from philosophical and natural historical works, as well as religious, poetic and biographical works. The questions discussed include: Do animals differ from humans intellectually? Were animals created for the use of humankind? Should animals be used for food, sport, or sacrifice? Can animals be our friends?

The selections are arranged thematically and, within themes, chronologically. A commentary precedes each excerpt, transliterations of Greek and Latin technical terms are provided, and each entry includes bibliographic suggestions for further reading.

Stephen T. Newmyer is Professor of Classics and Chair of the Department of Classics at Duquesne University in Pittsburgh. He has published widely on human–animal relations in classical thought, and is author of *Animals, Rights and Reason in Plutarch and Modern Ethics* (Routledge, 2006).

D1598712

Routledge Sourcebooks for the Ancient World

ANIMALS IN GREEK AND ROMAN THOUGHT

A sourcebook

Stephen T. Newmyer

Routledge
Taylor & Francis Group

LONDON AND NEW YORK

First published 2011
by Routledge
2 Park Square, Milton Park, Abingdon, Oxon OX14 4RN

Simultaneously published in the USA and Canada
by Routledge
270 Madison Ave, New York, NY 10016

Routledge is an imprint of the Taylor & Francis Group, an informa business

© 2011 Stephen T. Newmyer

The right of Stephen T. Newmyer to be identified as author of this work has
been asserted by him in accordance with sections 77 and 78 of the Copyright,
Designs and Patents Act 1988.

Typeset in Baskerville and Helvetica by Swales & Willis Ltd, Exeter, Devon
Printed and bound in Great Britain by CPI Antony Rowe, Chippenham, Wiltshire

British Library Cataloguing in Publication Data
A catalogue record for this book is available from the British Library

Library of Congress Cataloguing in Publication Data
Newmyer, Stephen Thomas.
Animals in Greek and Roman thought : a sourcebook /
by Stephen T. Newmyer.
p. cm.
Includes bibliographical references.
1. Animals–Greece–History. 2. Animals–Rome–History.
3. Animal rights–History. I. Title.
QL21.G8N49 2010
179'.3—dc22
2010019804

ISBN13: 978–0–415–77334–8 (hbk)
ISBN13: 978–0–415–77335–5 (pbk)
ISBN13: 978–0–203–83915–7 (ebk)

FOR RAE,

who helped me come back.

CONTENTS

CONTENTS

PREFACE

Since the rebirth of interest in the relationship between human and non-human animals that coincided, at least in the United States, with the flowering of such social causes as the Civil Rights Movement and Women's Liberation, an extraordinarily rich body of literature has been produced covering virtually every aspect of human–animal interaction.[1] Philosophers, zoologists, environmentalists, and animal activists of every description have argued passionately that non-humans share the faculty of reason that has for millennia been judged by many thinkers to be unique to human beings, that non-human animals therefore deserve to be included in the moral universe of their human counterparts, and that human treatment of animals should change in light of our kinship with non-human species. Others have argued with equal conviction that humans owe nothing to non-humans on the grounds that they have so little in common with human beings as to fall outside the bounds of human moral consideration.

For readers with an interest in the historical antecedents of modern debates on animal issues, a number of anthologies of what their compilers term the "classic" texts have appeared in recent years. Unfortunately, the term "classics" is frequently applied in anthologized collections to writings dating predominantly from the nineteenth and early twentieth centuries, with perhaps an occasional excerpt from Descartes and, in some instances, an offering from Thomas Aquinas or even the Old Testament. Greek and Roman "classics" are either omitted entirely or drastically underrepresented, despite the fact that virtually every subject encompassed in post-classical thought on human–animal relations was treated already in Greco-Roman authors, and that the Aristotelian and Stoic formulations of these arguments were instrumental in shaping much of subsequent thought on the nature of the animal estate.[2]

A number of reasons may be suggested for this underrepresentation of classical texts in available anthologies. Such collections have often been produced by philosophers active in the Animal Rights Movement or by social scientists who may be unfamiliar with the contributions of Greek and Roman thinkers. The ancient sources themselves present a variety of problems. Certain sources of primary importance to the study of ancient views on animals are highly fragmentary or survive only in testimonia embedded in the texts of writers even more obscure than the authors whom they cite, as in the case of references to Pythagoras or the Greek Stoics. Some fragmentary material has not been translated into English, while other authors whose writings on animals are critical to our understanding of the development of classical thought on animals, including Pliny the Elder, Plutarch and Porphyry, are often available only in scholarly editions intended primarily for the use of classicists.

The present volume is intended to fill the need for a selection of readings from Greek and Roman authors who discussed topics relating to human–animal interactions and who speculated on the nature of animalkind vis-à-vis humankind. The selections chosen come primarily from philosophical and natural historical works, although religious, poetic and biographical works are represented as well. With the exception of passages from the treatise *De animalibus* (*On Animals*) by the Jewish philosopher Philo of Alexandria, a work dating from the first century CE but extant only in Armenian translation,[3] I have translated all passages included in this volume. Since, in most cases, Greek and Roman authors touch upon topics relating to animals only in passing, in the context of works not devoted exclusively to such topics, some selections in this volume are quite brief. In those cases, I have attempted to offer sufficient context to make the selections comprehensible. The translations are intended solely to illuminate the meaning of the ancient texts in an accurate and clear manner, and have no literary pretensions. I use the word "animal" throughout this volume in the commonly understood meaning of that term to designate a non-human animal, and I attach no negative connotations of savagery or bestiality to the term.

Selections in this anthology are arranged by theme and, within themes, chronologically so that it may be possible for the reader to trace the development of classical thought on a given topic over time. I have endeavored to provide passages that illustrate arguments on both sides of every debate. A commentary precedes each excerpt or group of excerpts that serves to explain technical terms used by the author and that places excerpts within the context of classical thought on animals. I have included transliterations of Greek and Latin technical terms relating to complex philosophical concepts that might allow multiple translations and interpretations. Each entry includes bibliographic suggestions for further study on topics included in the entry. When relevant, I have included discussion of postclassical survivals and transformations of ideas presented in excerpts, especially as these are encountered in modern animal rights literature and in modern debate on the nature and limitations of animal cognition.

It is my hope that this anthology may prove useful to several audiences. Undergraduate and graduate philosophy and ethics courses, courses on all levels dealing with current environmental issues, courses in the history of science, and classics courses dealing with cultural aspects of antiquity may all find the volume serviceable. At the same time, general readers interested in arguments marshaled by partisans on both sides of the debate concerning animal rights may find the work helpful since the classical antecedents of these arguments tend to remain relatively unfamiliar to zealots on both sides.

Notes

1 On the historical connections between the so-called Animal Rights Movement and social causes in the United States, see Peter Singer, *Animal Liberation: A New Ethic for Our Treatment of Animals* (New York: Avon, 1975) 1–9 and Richard D. Ryder, *Animal Revolution: Changing Attitudes towards Speciesism* (Oxford: Blackwell, 1989) 2–6.

2 One such anthology of "classic" writings on animals, Tom Regan and Peter Singer, eds, *Animal Rights and Human Obligations* (Englewood Cliffs, NJ: Prentice Hall, 1976), contains only one passage from Aristotle and no other Greek or Roman text. Susan J. Armstrong and Richard G. Botzler, eds, *The Animal Ethics Reader* (London: Routledge, 2003) contains no text from Greek or Roman authors. Linda Kalof and Amy Fitzgerald, eds, *The Animals Reader* (Oxford: Berg-Palgrave, 2007) contains excerpts from Aristotle, Pliny and Plutarch.

3 Passages from Philo, *De animalibus*, are cited from Abraham Terian, *Philonis Alexandrini de Animalibus*, The Armenian Text with an Introduction, Translation, and Commentary (Chico, CA: Scholars Press, 1981). I would like to thank Professor Terian for his kind permission to include excerpts from his translation.

ACKNOWLEDGEMENTS

I would like to express my gratitude to Lalle Pursglove and to Matthew Gibbons at Routledge for their guidance and patience during the composition of this volume. I have profited immensely from their expertise. I owe special thanks to my departmental colleague Christine George, who never lost her patience and good spirits when I asked her to teach me yet again a computer function that she had taught me a thousand times before.

PRELIMINARY BIBLIOGRAPHIC NOTE

A number of works recommended in the suggestions for further reading that accompany the texts included in this anthology may be singled out here for providing especially useful overviews of ancient thought on a broad range of issues relating to animals as beings and to human–animal relations. Any reader interested in the place held by animals in the thought of the classical philosophical schools should consult the magisterial work of Richard Sorabji, *Animal Minds and Human Morals: The Origins of the Western Debate* (New York: Cornell University Press, 1993). Sorabji traces the consequences, in later philosophical thought, of Aristotle's denial of reason to non-human species, which inspired, especially after Stoicism added an ethical dimension to Aristotle's arguments, a long-lasting and detrimental anthropocentrism in Western thought that espoused the view that animals are intellectually inferior to human beings and therefore outside the sphere of human moral concern.

Equally rewarding is Urs Dierauer, *Tier und Mensch im Denken der Antike: Studien zur Tierpsychologie, Anthropologie und Ethik* (Amsterdam: Grüner, 1977). Dierauer investigates how Greek and Roman attitudes toward animals affected classical anthropology and ethics, giving special attention to the questions of what psychic capacities were ascribed to animals in ancient thought, how the ancients explained animal behavior, and in what respects animals were viewed as like or unlike human beings. He devotes attention primarily to philosophical texts, and leaves natural historical and poetic works largely outside of consideration.

Likewise anthropological in orientation, the anthology of Klaus Bartels, *Was Ist der Mensch: Texte zur Anthropologie der Antike* (Munich: Heimeran, 1975), offers, in German translation, a selection of texts from classical philosophers, historians, tragedians, and poets who attempt to define what "man" is, in some cases clarifying how "man" is to be differentiated from "animal." A minimal amount of explanatory commentary precedes most translated passages.

A number of the issues touched upon in the selections in this volume are discussed in the essays that make up Linda Kalof, ed., *A Cultural History of Animals in Antiquity* (Oxford and New York: Berg, 2007). Chapters on animals as symbols, as prey of hunters, as objects of domestication, as tools of the scientist, as material for philosophical speculation, as sources of entertainment, and as subjects for artists cover the period from 2500 BCE to 1000 CE, with the contributions of prehistoric, Egyptian and Mesopotamian cultures treated in addition to those of Greece and Rome.

Günther Lorenz, *Tiere im Leben der alten Kulturen: Schriftlose Kulture, Alter Orient, Ägypten, Griechenland und Rom* (Vienna: Böhlau, 2000) offers, in the third main section of his work, entitled "Die Gefühlsbeziehung zum Tier und die ersten Ansätze zum Tierschutz," a valuable discussion of the birth of an elementary understanding of what might be termed animal welfare in classical cultures. In Section III. 15, "Klassisches Griechenland," pp. 304–354, Lorenz surveys thinkers who maintained that human beings have ethical obligations toward animals, whether because of their belief in transmigration of souls or based on some other considerations, and thinkers who, like Aristotle and the Stoics, held that humans have no ethical obligations toward animals.

Two survey works tackle the knotty problem of what motivated certain segments of classical society to advocate or denigrate the vegetarian lifestyle. Johannes Haussleiter, *Der Vegetarismus in der Antike* (Berlin: Töpelmann, 1935), presents a comprehensive overview of ancient vegetarian thought from mythical-heroic times until the late fourth century CE, and offers a very brief discussion of the revival of vegetarianism in post-classical times with references to ancient texts that may have inspired thinkers of later ages to renounce meat-eating. Daniel A. Dombrowski, *The Philosophy of Vegetarianism* (Amherst, MA: University of Massachusetts Press, 1984), in contrast to Haussleiter, makes an effort to show how modern vegetarian thought grounds its position in philosophical arguments influenced by and in some cases derived from ancient antecedents.

A resource of enormous usefulness to anyone interested in the ancient encounter with animals is the extensive bibliography "Animals in Graeco-Roman Antiquity and Beyond," prepared by Thorsten Fögen and available online at www.telemachos.hu-berlin.de/esterni/Tierbibliographie_Foegen.pdf. This work, updated to May 2006, provides bibliographic citations of general works and studies devoted to individual animal species, including works concentrating on ethical, archaeological, zoological, legal and sociological aspects of the study of animals in the classical world.

Part I

ANIMALS AS BEINGS

1

THE INTELLECT OF ANIMALS: RATIONAL OR IRRATIONAL?

1. Alcmaeon of Croton

Alcmaeon of Croton in southern Italy (*c*.5th century BCE), famous for his researches on the human sense organs, especially the eye, is widely held to be the earliest Greek thinker who drew a sharp distinction between the intellectual capacities of human and non-human animals, and in so doing, he inaugurated the belief that man alone of animals is rational, a notion that became a fundamental assumption in much of subsequent classical speculation on animals. Likewise his distinction between understanding (*xunesis*) and perception (*aisthēsis*) would enjoy a long life in Greco-Roman thought. The natural consequence of an absence of rational capacity in non-human animals is, in Alcmaeon's view, a lack of language and an inability to advance culturally. It is reasonable to assume that Alcmaeon's researches on the human sense organs influenced his conclusions on animal mentality. The following statement on his views is derived from the treatise *On the Senses* by Theophrastus.

Animals Have No "Understanding"

For [Alcmaeon] says that man differs from the other creatures in that he alone has understanding (*xuniēsi*), while the other creatures have perception (*aisthanetai*), but do not have understanding.

("Alcmaeon," DK 1a)

2. Chrysippus

Chrysippus (*c*.280–207 BCE), head of the Stoic school of philosophy after Cleanthes, seems to have taken a particular interest in the intellectual capacities of animals, and he may have contributed substantially to the school's denial of reason to non-human species that would form the cornerstone of the school's position on animals. The *hēgemonikon*, or "governing principle," to which he alludes in this statement was held by the Stoics to be one of eight constituent parts of the soul in human and non-human animals, the other seven being the senses, the capacity for utterance and the capacity for reproduction. While this "governing principle" went on in human beings to attain to rationality, it remained forever irrational in non-humans, denying them the capacity for reason. Consequently, the actions of animals are, according to Stoic teaching, motivated merely by "impulse" (*hormē*), such as the tendency of an animal to move toward a food source and away from a source of danger or harm, neither action requiring the operation of reason. This intellectual disparity between humans and other species had wide-reaching consequences for the Stoics, the most fundamental of which was the elimination of any responsibility on the part of humans to consider the interests of animals in undertaking any action.

The *Hēgemonikon*, or "Governing Principle" in the Animal Soul Is Devoid of Reason

Every soul possesses a kind of "governing principle" (*hēgemonikon*), but [in animals] it is their life and sensation (*aisthēsis*) and impulse (*hormē*).

(SVF 2. 821)

3. Plato

The dialogues of Plato (*c.*429–347 BCE) reveal a broad familiarity with many species of animals, although Plato's interest in animals is more that of a metaphysician than of a biologist. Animals figure in his works rather frequently as metaphors and as images, and animality is quite often contrasted with humanity in Plato, to the disadvantage of animalkind: humans who do not live up to their potential as rational beings are likened to beasts that wallow in their lowliness, while those who remain uneducated are said to resemble the wildest of beasts (*Laws* 766a). Similarly, democratic government is said by Plato to be like a pack of animals that are impossible to control (*Republic* 563c). In common with a number of other ancient writers, he considered some kinds of animals, including bees and ants, to be positive models for human conduct, while others, such as wolves and lions, were emblematic of savagery and not to be emulated in human behavior.

Despite his fondness for metaphorical constructions of animality, it would be erroneous to claim that Plato had no scientific interest in animals. Although the criteria by which he distinguishes them are at times fanciful and unilluminating, he seems to have been interested in establishing a system of classification of animal species. He distinguishes animals at times according to their manner of breeding or feeding, but he never attains to any consistent position on division between species. Indeed, biologists tend to feel that Plato's playful and imaginative treatment of animals had in the final analysis a rather baneful influence on the progress of science, and he is not often accorded a place of honor in the ranks of Greek biologists.

One of the more intriguing appearances of animals in the Platonic corpus is found in the philosopher's doctrine of metempsychosis, usually understood to mean the transmigration of souls, a belief often associated with the pre-Socratic philosopher Pythagoras (6th century BCE). The doctrine of transmigration of souls is discussed in the *Phaedrus*, the *Republic*, the *Phaedo*, and the *Timaeus*, although these discussions do not agree in all details. In the *Phaedo*, Plato maintains (81e–82b) that humans may assume the form of other animal species through metempsychosis, depending upon their former manner of life: those who were gluttons and drunkards may become asses, while those who were unjust and tyrannical may pass into wolves or hawks. In contrast, those who displayed what he terms practical political virtues such as temperance and justice pass into gentle, "political" species such as ants or bees. In the *Republic*, however, a greater range of possibilities is explored (620d): some humans are said to choose a reincarnation that resembles their former mode of life, as Orpheus elected to be reborn as a swan and Aias as a lion. In this dialogue, animals are also envisioned as being capable of choosing to be reborn as human beings, as is said to be the case with swans. Similarly, he argues in the *Timaeus* that those individuals who did not allow their spiritual element to predominate entirely in their lifetimes will return as animals, and that the more irrationally an individual behaved in one life, the lowlier the animal species into which he will pass in his next incarnation (42c). The apparent lack of agreement in Plato's accounts has proved troubling to scholars since antiquity, and he allows Socrates to state (*Phaedo* 114d) that no reasonable person can take what he has described as incontrovertible fact, but it is remarkable how frequently the topic of transmigration of souls is encountered in the Platonic corpus. It also remains unclear what Plato believed happens to human reason when a person passes into an animal and, conversely, when an animal passes into a human. In the *Phaedrus* (249b), he sidesteps this problem altogether by declaring that only what had previously been a human soul can pass back into a human. In both the *Phaedrus* and the *Republic*, Plato discusses the punishments that some souls may expect in the afterlife, but this possibility is not broached in either the *Phaedo* or the *Timaeus*. The *Phaedo* also does not mention the possibility of animals passing into humans in their incarnations.

It is likewise difficult to assess Plato's position on the question of rationality in animals since he seems to waver in his views. While he frequently laments the fact that humans do not always make the effort to live completely rational lives and thereby to reach their potential, he generally considers animals to have intellectual powers far inferior to those of human beings. In the passages translated below, he seems to deny rationality to animals, but in the *Laws* (961d) he is willing to allow them a portion of intellect (*nous*).

The Animal Soul Is Irrational

[Socrates]: "All of this [Diotima] taught me when she would speak on the topic of love, and she asked, 'What, Socrates, do you suppose to be the cause of this love and desire? Do you not notice how powerfully all animals are acted upon when they are eager to reproduce, both land-dwelling and flying creatures, all of them lovesick and beset with desire, first to mate with one another and then to rear their offspring, and do you not notice that the weakest are willing to fight to the death against the strongest on behalf of their offspring and to die for them and be tortured with hunger in order to be able to feed their young, and to do anything else necessary? In the case of human beings,' she said, 'one might suppose they do all this from reason (*logismou*). But what is the cause of this erotic possession in the case of animals?'"

(Symposium 207a–c)

"But did you notice this?"

"What is that?"

"That what we just now thought about the spirited part (*thumoeidous*) of the soul is the opposite of what we now think? For then we supposed it was part of the appetitive (*epithumētikon*) soul, but now, far from it, we say that, in the factions of the soul, it takes up arms on the side of the rational (*logistikon*)."

"Undoubtedly."

"Well, is it then different from that also, or is it a form of the rational, so that there are not three but rather two forms of the soul, the rational and the appetitive? Or is it as in a city, that there are three types of structure: the moneymakers, the helpers, and the advisors, so that likewise in the case of the soul there is a third kind, the spirited (*thumoeides*), which is by nature the helper to the rational unless it is ruined by bad nurture?"

"It must be a third type."

"Yes indeed, if it is shown to be something different from the rational, just as it has been shown to be something different from the appetitive."

"That is not difficult to show. For one can see even in children that they are from birth full of spirit (*thumou*), whereas some seem to me at least never to take part in reason (*logismou*), while others do so rather late."

"Yes, by Zeus, you speak well. One can see that what you speak of is so in beasts as well."

(Republic 440e–441b)

4. Aristotle

Aristotle (384–322 BCE) is without question the most prolific and influential ancient writer to take up the questions of what constitutes the nature of animals, human and non-human, how human animals differ from non-human animals, how animals are to be classified, and how the intellectual properties of animals, human and non-human, are to be evaluated. While he at times employs analogy and simile in referring to the components of animal intellect, Aristotle avoids the highly developed and fanciful metaphorical language that is prominent in Plato's discussions of animals. His interest in animals is that of a biologist rather than of an ethical philosopher, and assertions that animals are morally inferior to human beings in consequence of their intellectual limitations are almost entirely absent in Aristotle. Later philosophical schools, in particular the Stoics, picked up on Aristotle's biological observations on differences between human and non-human animals and accorded to them a distinctly ethical interpretation, to the disadvantage of non-human species.

About one quarter of Aristotle's extant literary production is devoted to works of a biological nature. Such a preoccupation with life science was extraordinary in a pupil of Plato, and Aristotle defended his study of biology as a pursuit more closely connected to human life than was astronomy, a particular interest of the school of Plato, since humans live their own lives in close proximity to plants and animals while we can grasp relatively little notion of things above the earth, however noble they may be. Nor, he held, should humans think the study of the lowliest creatures ignoble, since even the smallest things have elements of the marvelous for those who take the time to look (*De partibus animalium* [*Parts of Animals*] 644b22–645a23).

The longest of Aristotle's treatises on animals, the so-called *Historia Animalium* (*History of Animals*), in ten books, is closest to a general treatment of zoology among his extant works. Heavily concerned with classification, reproduction and movement in animals, and somewhat loosely organized, the treatise contains some of Aristotle's most important pronouncements on animals, including an exposition of his theory of *sunecheia*, a sort of biological gradualism or continuity, by which nature advances from the simplest creatures to more sophisticated ones so gradually and almost imperceptibly that differences between species may appear infinitesimal (*History of Animals* 588b4–12). Nevertheless, nature still allowed for a distinct intellectual differentiation between human beings and other animal species in the matter of reason, which he denies to animals, although he allows that animals have "traces" (*ichnē*, *History of Animals* 588a20) of some human characteristics but only "resemblances" (*homoiotētēs*, *History of Animals* 588a24) of intelligence. Some have taken the doctrine of *sunecheia* to be an early statement of evolutionary theory, but this is incorrect since Aristotle believed in the permanence of genera and species. The latter books (VII–X) of the *Historia* have been considered to be at least in part the work of other individuals, including Aristotle's pupil Theophrastus (*c.*370–287 BCE), because they at times appear to contradict some of Aristotle's earlier-stated strictures concerning animal intellect; for example, memory (*mnēmē*) and thought (*dianoia*) are ascribed to animals in these latter books while they are denied them in the earlier books.

The treatise *De partibus animalium* (*Parts of Animals*), in four books, is concerned, as Aristotle explains it (*Parts of Animals* 646a10–12), with the question of what causes each animal to be as it is, that is to say, as he had described it in the *Historia*. More theoretical than the *Historia*, the work discusses the part played in the development of animals by factors that Aristotle designates as "causes" (*aitiai*): the "motive cause" in the production of a new organism, for example, is its parents; as "elements" (*dunameis*), of which Aristotle recognized the hot, the cold, the fluid and the dry (likely a borrowing from Presocratic speculation); and as "parts" (*moria*), which are further subdivided into "uniform parts," such as bone, blood and flesh, and "non-uniform parts," such as hands, faces and heads – if one were to cut up a bone, one would find smaller bits of bone, but if one were to cut up a face, one would not find a smaller face. These "parts" are described and characterized as they occur in various types of animals, including human beings, in the latter three books of the work. *Parts of Animals* also contains a statement of Aristotle's doctrine of teleology in the biological process, according to which the processes of life are goal-directed. Animals have the parts that they do to enable them to perform the functions for which they are designed. Human beings, for example, have hands because they, as nature's most intelligent beings, can make the best use of them (*Parts of Animals* 687a19–23). Modern science would consider this a statement of the idea that animals are generally well adapted to the sorts of lives that they lead.

The five books entitled *De generatione animalium* (*Generation of Animals*) discuss reproduction in animal and include a presentation of Aristotle's doctrine of the four causes (final, formal, efficient and material) which determine the origin, character and end toward which animals advance.

Both *De motu animalium* (*Movement of Animals*) and *De incessu animalium* (*Locomotion of Animals*), each in one book, are, like *Generation of Animals*, somewhat theoretical in their approach to their subjects, especially so in the case of *Movement of Animals*. This work takes up the subject of the "prime mover," a distinct, external unmoved force that brings movement to other entities. *Locomotion of Animals* is concerned with the sorts of movements of which animals are capable, and much attention is given to the processes of flexion in animal limbs.

Aristotle also had occasion to discuss animals in treatises not specifically dedicated to biological topics. He viewed the soul (*psuchē*) as a biological rather than a spiritual entity, intimately connected to the body in which it dwelled and not existing outside of a body, and he did not deny soul to plants or animals. In *De anima* (*On the Soul*), Aristotle defined *psuchē* as the "actuality" (*entelecheia*) of a body (*On the Soul* 412a20–22), the capacity that gives an entity its life. Plants are said to have "nutritive" souls that enable them to use food to maintain their bodily structure. The souls of animals are more developed and have, in addition to the nutritive element, consciousness (*aisthēsis*) and locomotion, but they do not possess reason (*nous*), which is unique to the human soul. Since, unlike his teacher Plato, Aristotle held that souls have no existence separate from bodies (*On the Soul* 414a19), he did not accept the concept of transmigration of souls.

Scholars have maintained that Aristotle seems at times to attribute intellectual capacities to animals in his biological works that he denies to them in his more anthropocentric works such as the *Politics* and the *Nicomachean Ethics* and *Eudemian Ethics*, and this has led some to charge him with inconsistency. Moreover, it appears that he uses some technical terms, such as *phronēsis*, a kind of "practical wisdom," and *sunesis*, "understanding," in senses both synonymous and somewhat different when referring to animals than when referring to the intellectual capacities of humans. He also repeatedly employs phrases such as "just as" and "somewhat like" to compare human and animal capacities, which tends to blur his meaning. Most notably, however, Aristotle's assertions that because humans have so little in common with animals, they can stand in no relation of justice with them (*Nicomachean Ethics* 1161a30–1162b2) and that animals were intended for man's use (*Politics* 1256b15–26), have led him to be charged with speciesism – the tendency to value human beings over the remainder of animal creation. One may perhaps defend Aristotle by noting that his intention in such assertions was more to understand the place of man in creation than to disparage other animal species. His observations appear to be strictly biological in intent. The majority of Aristotle's pronouncements on the content of the intellect of animals suggest that he considered them to lack reason (*logos*), the capacity to think rationally (*logismos*) and thought (*dianoia*). He does, however, allow them some form of the abovementioned *phronēsis*, which is usually considered to be a form of "practical wisdom" that enables animals to cope successfully with the demands of their environment and that he believed to exist in varying degrees within animal species.

Biological Gradualism or Continuity

Hence nature passes from inanimate beings to animals little by little, so that, as a result of the continuity (*sunecheia*), that which constitutes the border between them and the middle of them escapes our notice. After inanimate beings come first the classes of plants. Among these, one differs from another in seeming to have more of a share of life, and the entire class, compared with other bodies, seems almost animate, but compared with animals, it appears inanimate. For the change from them to the animate is, as was stated before, continuous.

(Historia Animalium [History of Animals] 588b4–12)

Ascidia (Sea-squirts) differ in nature from plants, but still they are more animal-like than are sponges, for they have altogether the character of a plant. For nature passes continuously from the inanimate to the animate, moving through living creatures that are not animals, in such a way that there seems to be little difference altogether from one to the next.

(De partibus animalium [Parts of Animals] 681a10–15)

Only Man Is Deliberative

Some [animals] are knavish and mischievous, like the fox, and others are high-spirited and affectionate and fawning, like the dog, while others are gentle and readily tamed, like the elephant. Some are bashful and wary, like the goose, and others jealous and preening, like the peacock. But only man is deliberative (*bouleutikon*). Many animals share in memory and teachability, but none but man has the power of recollection.

(History of Animals 488a20–26)

Humans Differ from Animals Intellectually

This is then the nature of animals in other respects and in their birth. Their actions and lifestyles differ in accord with their characters and nourishment. For in most other animals there are traces of those things that pertain to the characteristics of the soul, things which demonstrate more obvious differences in the case of human beings. For tameness and fierceness, gentleness and harshness, courage and cowardice, fears and acts of bravery, boldness and trickery, and resemblances of understanding (*suneseōs*) are in many [animals], just as we spoke of with respect to bodily parts. Some characteristics differ in a "more or less" relationship with human beings, as does man in comparison with animals (for some of these characteristics are present in a greater degree in humans, and some in the other animals), and others differ by analogy. Just as there are in humans technological skill, wisdom (*sophia*) and understanding (*sunesis*), so there exists in some animals another natural capacity (*dunamis*) of such a sort. Such a phenomenon is most evident if we examine the age of childhood, for in children it is possible to see traces, as it were, and seeds of the permanent dispositions that will arise in them, but in this time period their soul does not differ at all, one might say, from that of animals, so it is not unreasonable if some characteristics are alike, some similar, and some analogous to those of other animals.

(History of Animals 588a16–18–588b3)

Reason Is What Distinguishes Man

Being alive seems to be shared even by plants, but we are seeking that which is unique [to man]. Now, we must put aside life functions of nutrition and growth. Some sort of sentient (*aisthētikē*) life would follow next. This too seems to be common to a horse and to a cow and to every beast. There remains, then, one practical (*praktikē*) life of him who possesses reason.

(Nicomachean Ethics 1097b33–1098a4)

Only Man Is Rational

Now other animals live largely by nature (*phusei*), but some in small respects live by their habits also. Man lives by reason as well, for he alone possesses reason. Hence it is necessary that these things harmonize with one another [in man] since men frequently act contrary to their acquired habits and nature on account of their reason if they believe that some other behavior is better.

(Politics 1332b3–8)

Mental Capacities of Humans and Animals Compared

By nature, animals are born with sensation (*aisthēsin*); from this arises memory in some of them but not in others. For this reason, the former are more possessed of practical wisdom (*phronimōtera*) and more readiness to learn than the latter which are not capable of memory. Those animals that cannot hear sounds, like the bee and other such creatures, have practical wisdom but not the capacity to learn. Creatures that have this sense along with memory are capable of learning.

Now, all animals live by impressions (*phantasiais*) and memories, and have a small share of experience. The human race lives by skill and reason. Men acquire experience from memory, for many memories of the same thing end up having the force of one experience. Experience seems very much like knowledge and skill, but knowledge and skill arise from experience among human beings.

(Metaphysics 980a28–981a4)

5. Philo of Alexandria

The Jewish philosopher Philo of Alexandria (1st century CE) is generally considered to be the author of the dialogue known by the Latin title *De animalibus* (*On*

Animals) but whose Greek title translates as *Alexander, or Whether Dumb Animals Possess Reason*. The Greek original of the treatise is lost with the exception of the Greek title and a few fragments of the text, but the work survives in an Armenian translation that appears to date from some period between the sixth and eighth centuries CE and seems to have been produced for the use of Armenian students who intended to study in Byzantine seminaries. Scholars familiar with the Armenian language observe that the translation is syntactically awkward, at times almost unintelligible, apparently from an attempt to reproduce the word order of the Greek original, and full of lengthy circumlocutions occasioned by a lack of precise Armenian equivalents for the Greek vocabulary. No doubt because of the unusual state of its preservation, and despite its inherent interest as one of only a handful of classical works devoted entirely to philosophical discussion of animals, the treatise attracted little scholarly attention until it appeared in a faculty Latin translation in 1822. It received its first translation into a modern language in the superb English edition, with Armenian text and exhaustive commentary, by Abraham Terian in 1981.[1]

The *De animalibus* purports to be an oral reading by Philo's grandnephew Lysimachus of the text of a lecture that Philo had heard delivered by his nephew Alexander, who is named in the original Greek title of the treatise. Lysimachus asks Philo to comment on the lecture at the end of the reading. Sections 10–71 of the work contain Alexander's defense of the proposition that animals possess reason, a position that he bolsters with examples in animals of apparently rational activity of a sort familiar from Greek and Roman authors who argued for rationality in animals, including, for example, Plutarch, Porphyry, and the cataloguer of animal wonders, Aelian. Following Lysimachus' recitation of Alexander's arguments, Philo offers a rebuttal in Sections 77–100 that is rather brief, general in nature, and surprisingly spiritless in view of Philo's aversion to the ideas presented in Alexander's exposition. Philo argues partially from a religious point of view, maintaining that to advance the idea that animals possess reason raises them to the level of human beings, an impious notion, and thereby risks sacrilege. Of the following excerpts, only the last is derived from Philo's rebuttal, and illustrates his strong rejection, influenced by Stoic arguments against rationality in animals, of Alexander's position.

A number of ideas prominent in classical discussions of animal intellect vis-à-vis that of human beings are at least hinted at in Alexander's exposition. Those who are said in Sections 11–12 to refuse to attribute any degree of reason to animals are the Stoics. Alexander's reference there to two kinds of reason is an allusion to the distinction made forcefully by the Stoics between what was termed *logos endiathetos*, what Alexander calls "the one located in the mind," and *logos prophorikos*, what Alexander terms "uttered reason." The former of these may be translated as "inner reason," and is roughly equivalent to "thought," which exercises control over and accords vocal expression to the other sort of reason, which may be termed "uttered reason" or "meaningful speech." In Stoic doctrine, the capacity for meaningful speech arises in the so-called *hēgemonikon*, a part of the soul in human and non-human animals that becomes rational in humans but remains irrational in non-humans. In consequence, *logos endiathetos*, or "thought," is impossible for non-humans, and their uttered expressions are without meaning (see also below, pp. 59–69, on language in animals). Alexander maintains, on the contrary, that animals possess both types of reason to some degree. He alludes once again to the concept of the *hēgemonikon* in Section 29, when he speaks of a "sovereign mind."

The allusion to upright posture in humans in contrast to the stance of other animals that compels them to face the earth is an instance of a philosophical commonplace repeated in almost endless forms in classical discussions on animals, and which might be called the "man alone of animals" argument. It is variously alleged that man alone of animals can laugh, experience the divine, be happy, feel emotions, use tools, count and even indulge in sexual activity all year long. The claim of uniqueness of human posture is found, among other places, in Xenophon, *Memorabilia* I. 4. 13; Plato, *Timaeus* 91e–92a; and Aristotle, *Parts of Animals* 686a27.

In Section 17, Alexander alludes, in comments again directed primarily against the Stoics, to the notion frequently encountered in ancient advocates of the position that animals are endowed with reason to some degree, that that capacity is proven by observation of the remarkable behavior of such creatures as ants, bees and some birds including swallows, all of which could not perform the intricate home-constructing activities that we can observe if they were not endowed with some degree of reason. Opponents of this position maintained, to the contrary, that such activities illustrated merely the activity of what these opponents termed *phusis*, which scholars have taken to mean instinct.

Alexander's tale of the dog that appeared to deliberate on which path to take in pursuing prey (Section 45) is a retelling of the frequently repeated anecdote of the Stoic Chrysippus, otherwise no supporter of the concept of rationality in animals, who observed that a certain dog appeared to be capable of syllogistic logic. Chrysippus probably considered that the dog merely carried out some action that was analogous to rational evaluation of opposite possibilities, and was not in fact capable of true reasoning at all, although Alexander does not suggest alternative explanations that might not require rationality.

In his rather flaccid response to the arguments presented in Alexander's lecture, Philo concedes that animals may demonstrate such traits as courage in a degree higher than one experiences in human beings, a fact that anyone after all can plainly see and which was often granted to animals by their ancient opponents, but he refuses to allow them any capacities that would suggest the presence of reason. In so arguing, he employs a version of the "man alone of animals" stance, maintaining that only man can understand God, government, or law. In the final section of the treatise (100), Philo warns readers to beware of subscribing to the arguments of Alexander because one thereby risks sacrilege by elevating animals to the exalted position occupied by humans in God's universe. It is interesting to note that even here, Philo argues as much from a Stoic position as from the position of his own Jewish faith, since it was a tenet of Stoicism as well as of biblical teaching that humans and animals did not stand on the same level in the scheme of creation because animals are, after all, irrational in the Stoic view of the natural world.[2]

Evidences of Rationality in Animals and Objections to That Position

Just as men ignore the weakness of women – as is common in every community whether in times of war or peace – and subjugate them only to themselves, considering the disadvantaged female sex unfit for state affairs, so, I think, when humans saw all the dumb animals bending downward to the earth, whereas they themselves stood upright and erect upon the ground, they differentiated between their own good attributes and the condition of the dumb animals. And since their minds were elevated as well as their bodies, they held the earthly creatures in disdain. Reason is the best of things that exist, but they attributed none of it to animals. Rather they appropriated it to themselves as though they had received an irreversible reward from nature. Since man possesses reason, he may refute a fallacy by disproving it: because of his ability to learn and his desire to discern clearly, he will discover truth.

However there are two kinds of reason: the one located in the mind is like a spring which issues from the sovereign part of the soul, whereas uttered reason is like a stream which, in the natural usage, courses over the lips and tongue and on to the sense of hearing. But although both kinds of reason appear to be imperfect in animals, they are none the less fundamental.

(De animalibus [On Animals] 11–12)

It seems to me that the friends of truth are not at all concerned about the beautiful and do not acknowledge unanimously that the faculty of reason is implanted in every creature endowed with a soul. Would that someone would consider this clear proof. Is not the spider very proficient in making various designs? Have you not observed how it works and what an amazing thing it fashions? For who else works as hard at spinning or weaving? I am not talking ironically but comparatively. Who rates second in art? Even those who from childhood are neither listless nor careless in their pursuit of art are actually surpassed or outdone. Taking a useless substance, as though it were wool, it fashions it in a very skillful and artistic manner. First it spins it very thin, as though by hand. Then by stretching and intertwining, spinning and weaving so wonderfully, it is capable to creating a fine piece of art to make open space look like lace. With enduring patience it weaves back and forth, wisely having in mind a lyre with its curves and circular shape – the circular is always more durable than the straight. A clear proof is that when the wind blows from every direction and things pile up one on top of another, it hardly ever becomes torn.

(On Animals 17)

Thus nature has planted a sovereign mind in every soul. In some it has a very faint imprint, an inexplicable and ill-defined form of an image; in others it has the likeness of a well-defined, very distinct, and fastidiously clear image; and still in others it is of an indistinct kind. But the deep and distinct impressions are borne upon the image of man.

(On Animals 29)

A hound was after a beast. When it came to a deep shaft which had two trails beside it – one to the right and the other to the left, and having but a short distance yet to go, it deliberated which way would be worth taking. Going to the right and finding no trace, it returned and took the other. Since there was no clearly perceptible mark there either, with no further scenting it jumped into the shaft to track down hastily. This was not achieved by chance but rather by deliberation of the mind.

(On Animals 45)

Now each has attained its share. It is obvious that not only men but also various other animals have inherited the faculty of reason. Furthermore it is believed that they possess both virtues and vices. An excuse is considerately made for those who have neither heard such a subject nor studied it on their own and so have remained in ignorance. But to those who have been endowed by God and natural agencies with fundamentals of knowledge and who have been instructed orally, it is fair to speak angrily as to laggards and enemies of truth.

(On Animals 71)

We agree that there are some decent and good qualities which are applicable to animals and many other functions which help preserve and maintain their courage; these are observed by sight. There is certainly in everything perceived or discerned in all the various species. But surely animals have no share of reasoning ability, for reasoning ability extends itself to a multiplicity of abstract concepts in the mind's perception of God, the universe, laws, provincial practices, the state, state affairs, and numerous other things, none of which animals understand.

(On Animals 85)

6. Seneca

The Roman Stoic philosopher Lucius Annaeus Seneca (*c.*4 BCE–65 CE), often called the Younger to distinguish him from his like-named father, a Spanish rhetorician, came to Rome and was appointed tutor to the young Nero, in which post he worked, at first successfully, to guide the wayward future emperor. His numerous works include a number of ethical treatises, seven books of *Naturales Quaestiones* (*Natural Questions*), which examine scientific issues from a Stoic point of view and have a moralizing bent, tragedies in verse, and the *Epistulae Morales* (*Moral Letters*), 124 letters, in reality short moral essays, addressed to his friend Gaius Lucilius. Most of Seneca's observations on animals are found in these letters.

Although it is frequently stated that Seneca inherited and espoused a milder brand of Stoicism, developed in part by Posidonius of Apamea (*c.*135–*c.*51 BCE), Seneca's pronouncements on animals in the *Moral Letters* do not seem radically different from those of such hard-line Stoics as Chrysippus who denied reason to non-human animals and held that humans have no kinship with them nor any obligation of justice toward them. In the following passage from *Letter* 76, Seneca develops the argument frequently encountered in ancient philosophers who opposed attributing reason to animals that, while other animal species may excel humans in some physical traits, reason is the exclusive possession of human beings.

Reason Distinguishes Man

All things are valued according to that which is good in them. Its fertility recommends the vine, its speed the stag. One asks how strong the backs of pack animals are, whose sole use is to bear burdens. In the case of the dog, keenness of smell is of primary importance if it is to search out wild creatures. If it is to catch prey, it needs speed; it needs courage if it is to rip into and harass that prey. In each thing, that quality should be best for which the creature is born and by which it is judged. What is best in a human being? Reason. In this he excels animals, and is excelled by the gods. Perfect reason is the good peculiar to men. All other qualities are common enough to him and animals. He is strong: so are lions. He is handsome: so are peacocks. He is swift: so are horses. I do not maintain that he is surpassed in all of these features. I do not ask what is greatest in man, but what is his own. He has body: so do trees. He has impulse and voluntary movement: so do beasts and worms. He has a voice, but how much louder is that of the dog, how much sharper that of the eagle, how much deeper that of the bull, and how much more flexible that of the nightingale. What is specific to man? Reason. This, when correct and complete, makes his happiness total. Thus, if each thing is praiseworthy when it has brought its own good to perfection and it has reached the end called for by its nature, and if man's own good is reason, a man is then praiseworthy if he has perfected his reason and he has reached the end called for by his nature. This perfect reason is virtue and is likewise that which is honorable.

(*Moral Letters* 76. 8–10)

7. Plutarch

Plutarch (*c*.50–120 CE) is most familiar to modern readers as the author of twenty-three pairs of *Parallel Lives*, biographies of Greek and Roman political figures whose careers allow him to draw edifying comparisons on their conduct and character. His interest in ethical issues was developed further in the more than seventy treatises known collectively by the not very informative term *Moralia* (*Moral Discourses*). Many of the works included in this collection are cast in the form of dialogues that for the most part do not reflect the Platonic manner of true argument and exchange of ideas but consist often of sometimes lengthy set speeches by the interlocutors. The subject matter of the treatises included in the *Moralia* is remarkably diverse, ranging from discourses on religious questions to dinner conversations, to treatises offering advice on interpersonal relationships.

Among the most fascinating of these treatises are three dealing with human–animal relationships. The longest and most carefully argued of these is known by its somewhat misleading Latin title *De sollertia animalium* (*On the Cleverness of Animals*), ostensibly a comparison of the "cleverness" of land-dwelling animals and marine animals, but in fact a defense of the position that all animals possess some degree of reason, the thesis of the dialogue that is set forth in the first excerpt from Plutarch below (*On the Cleverness of Animals* 960A–B). This and the other intellectual attributes that Plutarch ascribes to animals enable them, he argues, to cope successfully with their lives and entitle them to respectful treatment from human beings, if possession of reason is to be considered a prerequisite for entrance into the sphere of human moral concern, as was frequently demanded in ancient philosophical discussions of human–animal relations. The essentially artificial division of animals into land-dwelling and sea-dwelling for comparison in the dialogue suggests that Plutarch's real interest lay elsewhere than in mere comparison, and much of the work is in fact devoted to development of the idea that human beings stand in an ethical relation with all animals based on the intellectual capacities that he has attempted to demonstrate in them.

The amusing dialogue known both as *Bruta animalia ratione uti* (*Whether Beasts Are Rational*) and as *Gryllus* ("*Oinker*," "*Squeaker*"), from the name of one of the interlocutors, an eloquent pig, is a satiric recasting of the Circe episode of *Odyssey* X. In Plutarch's reworking, Odysseus wishes to intercede with the witch Circe to convince her to reconvert his men into humans after she has turned them into pigs. Gryllus declines on the grounds that life as an animal is in every respect preferable to the miserable existence of human beings. In this work, Gryllus espouses the position, otherwise unparalleled in the works of Plutarch and in contradiction to his pronouncements elsewhere, that animals are in fact superior to human beings in their behavior in that they live in accord with nature (*phusis*), which is their teacher in virtues such as temperance and courage, qualities which humans must learn from others and generally subvert in the course of their lives.

The third of Plutarch's treatises on animals, *De esu carnium* (*On the Eating of Flesh*), is an impassioned and at times grisly defense of the vegetarian lifestyle based on religious, ethical and hygienic grounds. This work, in two parts, survives in a somewhat mutilated state.

Topics relating to animals are touched upon as well in other treatises included in the *Moralia* that are devoted in large measure to other subjects. In *De amore prolis* (*On the Love of Offspring*), Plutarch maintains that non-human animals love their offspring as tenderly as do human parents, although in that work, he contradicts the position that he advances in *On the Eating of Flesh* by arguing that the sense of justice is less well developed in non-human species than in human beings. He also makes the interesting point there that animals live more in accord with nature (*phusis*) and are less given to corrupt and excessive behaviors than are their human counterparts. He naturally has occasion to touch upon questions relating to dietary choices in such works as *De tuenda sanitate praecepta* (*On Precepts for Maintaining Health*) and *Quaestiones Convivalium* (*Table Talk*).

Among Plutarch's many claims to the attention of the reader interested in ancient views on animals is the fact that he is one of few extant authors who devoted entire treatises to aspects of the topic, and one of very few ancient authors who were willing to argue that animals possess reason to some degree. In Plutarch's view, animals differ *quantitatively* rather than *qualitatively* in their capacity for reason from one animal species to another and between non-human and human animals (*On the Cleverness of Animals* 963A).

Some of the arguments upon which Plutarch builds his case for rationality in animals are of a sort that might be labeled "common-sensical": why, he asks, would hunters bother to pit themselves against animals if they did not judge their prey to be worthy adversaries whose intellectual endowments are sufficiently developed as to make the hunt a real test of wits (*On the Cleverness of Animals* 966A)? How would animals know how to build nests or webs or to rear offspring or to choose one path in preference to another if they did not have a sufficient share of reason to enable them to carry out these operations (*On the Cleverness of Animals* 966E, 969B–C)? Plutarch argued, principally against the Stoics, that it is absurd to maintain that creatures not designed by nature to display the perfection of reason therefore have no reason at all. Perfect reason, after all, is scarcely to be isolated even in human beings, and in them it is the result of much care and education (*On the Cleverness of Animals* 962C).

Plutarch employed Aristotle's notion that nature does everything toward some end to counter certain aspects of the Stoic case against attributing rationality to non-human animals. That school had advanced a "theory of opposites," set forth in the treatise *On Opposites* by Chrysippus (see pp. 3–4), according to which properties in nature are counterbalanced by their opposites. The mortal, for example, must be counterbalanced by the immortal, the destructible by the indestructible, and, naturally enough, the rational by the irrational. The non-human animal kingdom constitutes that irrational opposite, in Stoic theory, to rational humankind. Plutarch argued that, while no one would deny that all things that are soulless are irrational, even the Stoics agree that all animals have souls, and all besouled creatures are sentient. All sentient creatures must be endowed with reason because nature would not endow any creature with sentience without intending it to put that sentience to some use. Sentient creatures know how to flee their enemies and pursue their prey, to tell the useful from the harmful, and to hope, fear, desire and remember. All of these functions presuppose some degree of reason.

In the opening sections of Plutarch's dialogue *On the Cleverness of Animals*, wherein the dramatic scene is laid out for the reader, the character Autobulus, apparently Plutarch's own father, reminds the other interlocutors that on the previous day a lecture in praise of hunting had been read aloud which, he fears, may inflame young persons to take up arms against animals. He and Soclarus, a family friend of Plutarch, then engage in an extended philosophical debate (*On the Cleverness of Animals* 959A–965D) on the question of whether non-human animals are endowed with reason. Autobulus makes the case that animals are endowed with reason, while Soclarus advances the Stoic-inspired argument that they are not. In the remaining thirty chapters of the work, the intellectual endowments of land-dwelling and sea-dwelling animals are compared by the characters Aristotimus and Phaedimus. Neither group is finally judged to be more "clever."

Evidences of Rationality in Animals Drawn from Their Behavior

AUTOBULUS: By expressing the view yesterday, as you know, that all animals share, in some way or another, in thought (*dianoias*) and reason (*logismou*), we provided our young hunters a pleasant and delightful subject for debate, namely that of the intelligence of land-dwelling *versus* sea-dwelling creatures. It seems we shall decide this issue if the adherents of Aristotimus and Phaedimus stand by their challenges. The former offered to be the advocate for the position that the land engenders creatures with superior intelligence, the latter that the sea does so.

(*De sollertia animalium* [*On the Cleverness of Animals*] 960A–B)

SOCLARUS: There is plenty of the irrational in all things that do not have a share of soul, and we need no other counterpart to the rational; but everything that is soulless, insofar as it is without reason and understanding, is opposite to that which has reason and thought, along with a soul.

(*On the Cleverness of Animals* 960C)

AUTOBULUS: But he is foolish who seeks both the sentient and the nonsentient in besouled creatures, or who seeks both that which possesses mental images (*phantasmioumenon*) and does not, since every besouled creature possesses sentience and mental images from birth, so he will not reasonably demand both the rational and the irrational among besouled creatures, since he is arguing against persons who believe that nothing has a share of sensation that does not also have a share of understanding (*suneseōs*) and that there is no living creature that does not by nature possess some sort of opinion (*doxa*) and reason, just as it possesses sensation and impulse (*hormē*). For nature, which men rightly say does everything for a purpose, does not make a creature sentient just to sense when something happens to it. Since there are many things that are friendly (*oikeion*) to it and many that are alien, it would not live for a moment if it had not learned to be on guard against some and to associate with others. Sensation gives each creature the knowledge of both in equal measure. Yet there would be no mechanism, in creatures not born to reason and judge and remember and pay heed, to allow for the seizure that follows upon the recognition of the useful and the avoidance and shunning of the dangerous and painful.

(*On the Cleverness of Animals* 960D–E)

GRYLLUS: Who [taught] Cretan goats, when they fall victim to arrows, to seek out dittany, after eating which the arrows fall out? If you speak the truth, namely that nature is their teacher, you elevate the wisdom (*phronēsis*) of beasts to the most exalted and wisest of first principles. If you do not think this should be called reason (*logismon*) or understanding, it is time that you seek out a fairer and more worthy name for it, since clearly it brings into play a force which is better and more wondrous.

(*Gryllus, or Bruta animalia ratione uti* [*Whether Beasts Are Rational*] 991F)

GRYLLUS: Nightingales teach their nestlings to sing, whereas those caught while still young and reared by human hands sing in an inferior manner, as if they had left their instructor too soon … And having come into this body, I wonder at the reasonings by which I was convinced to believe that all creatures but man are irrational and mindless.

ODYSSEUS: Well, Gryllus, [now that] you are transformed, does even a sheep or an ass seem rational to you?

GRYLLUS: From these [very beasts], excellent Odysseus, one can best judge that by their nature animals are not without their share of reason (*logou*) and understanding (*suneseōs*); for just as it is not the case that one tree is more or less soulless than another, since all are alike with respect to their being senseless (for none has a soul), so likewise one animal would not seen more inert or dull-witted than another if they did not all have a share of reason and understanding somehow, one more or less than another.

(*Whether Beasts Are Rational* 992 B–D)

8. Aelian

Claudius Aelianus (Aelian) (170–235 CE) was by trade a rhetorician who possessed an unusually developed interest in animals. In his extant work *De natura animalium* (*On the Nature of Animals*), in seventeen books, he relates innumerable fascinating anecdotes that purport to illustrate the operation of divine providence in the lives of animals. As is the case with the works of other ancient cataloguers of the marvelous and paradoxical whose interest lay in offering moralizing observations about human behavior that might be derived from comparison and contrast with animal behavior, there is little evidence in Aelian of first-hand observation of the activities of animals. Aelian's account of the reaction of the Stoic philosopher Cleanthes (331–232 BCE) to the behavior of ants is typical of his tendency to draw moral lessons from his material. While Cleanthes, as a Stoic, might have been expected to deny the presence of reason in non-human species, Aelian suggests that the philosopher believed the ants capable of comprehending, in some elemental form, the concept of justice and of operating according to that comprehension, since they paid a "ransom" for the body of one of their comrades. This act calls forth Aelian's indignant comment about the poet Hesiod, who argued (*Opera et Dies* [*Works and Days*] 277–280) (translated below, p. 83) that Zeus did not give a sense of justice to animals other than man.

Cleanthes Judged Ants To Be Rational

This story, they say, compelled Cleanthes of Assos to yield a point to animals, against his will, and to give up his position that animals are without reason (*logismou*). Cleanthes happened to be sitting and resting for a while. There were numerous ants around his feet. He observed that some of them were carrying a dead ant along a certain path to the dwelling of some other ants that were not their nestmates. He observed that they stopped at the rim of the nest with the dead body and that other ants came up from below and met them, apparently for some purpose. This happened repeatedly. He stated that eventually they brought up a worm, as a ransom, it seemed. The others accepted it and handed over the dead body. They received it willingly, as if they were carrying off the body of a son or a brother. What would Hesiod say to this when he argued that Zeus made a distinction between animal natures and asserted that "fish and beasts and winged birds devour each other, for there is no justice among them, but [Zeus] gave justice to mankind"? Priam would not agree with this, since he, a human being and a descendant of Zeus, ransomed back Hector at the price of many spectacular treasures, from a man who was a hero and likewise the descendant of Zeus.

(*On the Nature of Animals* VI. 50)

9. Porphyry

The Neoplatonist philosopher Porphyry (234–c.305 CE), born at Tyre in Phoenicia, is the author of one of the most valuable documents relating to human–animal relations to survive from the ancient world – the four-book treatise known by the Latin title *De abstinentia* (*On Abstinence from Animal Flesh*), in which virtually every argument advocating the vegetarian lifestyle, from philosophical to ethical to hygienic to anatomical considerations, is discussed. The treatise takes the form of a long letter to Porphyry's friend Firmus Castricius, who had followed a vegetarian lifestyle but had reverted to meat eating, that seeks to show him the error of his ways.

Although Book III, which presents Porphyry's case for the presence of reason (*logos*) in animals and for a consequent debt of justice on the part of human beings to non-human animals, has garnered the most attention from scholars – all four books contain material of considerable interest. The opening book presents arguments raised in ancient literature that oppose the adoption of a vegetarian lifestyle, including the notion that animals seek to harm human beings and eating them controls their natural tendency toward over-breeding (I. 4). Book II deals at length with the issue of animal sacrifice, a central feature of the religious practice of most ancient societies. As an advocate of abstinence from meat eating, Porphyry asks in the latter half of Book II if the gods might not welcome grain offerings that involve no violence instead of slain animals (II. 33–61). The fourth book discusses other ancient groups who practiced abstinence from meat, including the Egyptian priesthood, the Jewish Essenes, and the Indian Brahmans.

Book III strives to counter the Stoic position that animals are irrational and that humans have therefore no obligation toward them to abstain from using them in any way that benefits humans. Porphyry counters that the true philosopher has an obligation to refrain from causing harm to others, not least because non-human animals are, in contrast to the position of the Stoics, in possession of at least some degree of rationality (III. 7). The philosopher demonstrates this rationality through various examples, including their evident ability to regulate their lives successfully: they build nests, they raise their young, they avoid their enemies and pursue their prey, and they even express themselves in complex utterances. The fact that humans cannot understand animal utterances does not, in Porphyry's view, argue against their constituting a language since Greek speakers do not understand the utterances of the Indians or of the Thracians but would not therefore claim that they do not use language (III. 3. 4).

Porphyry agrees with the predecessor Plutarch, from whom he copies almost verbatim for long stretches (Book III. 3. 20. 7–III. 24. 5), that rationality in animals is a matter of quantity rather than quality (III. 7. 1). In consequence, if animals fulfill the Stoic requirement that humans can owe justice only to those who are like humans, one cannot deny justice to non-human animals. In contrast to Plutarch, however, Porphyry's position on justice toward animals was heavily colored by his Platonist conviction that the true philosopher needed to avoid acts of injustice against those who were harmless lest that behavior taint the human's search for spiritual goodness. It could be argued that, in the final analysis, Porphyry's seemingly generous and enlightened position toward animals was motivated to some extent by selfish considerations of personal purity rather than by concern for animals as conscious beings. This possibility seems to find some support in Porphyry's assertion (III. 3) that not all humans are bound to follow a life of abstinence but only those who seek to attain to the true philosophical life.

Arguments for Rationality in Animals

However, if we may believe Aristotle, animals have been seen teaching their offspring not just to do other things but also to speak, as the nightingale teaches her nestling to speak. And as he himself says, animals learn many things from each other and likewise many things from human beings. Everyone bears witness that he speaks the truth, every horsebreaker and groomer and rider and charioteer, and every hunter and elephant driver and herdsman and all trainers of wild animals and birds. A sensible person allows a share of understanding (*suneseōs*) to animals on the basis of such evidences, while the thoughtless person who has done no study of these things is carried astray, supported by his own arrogance toward animals. How can he not speak ill of creatures that he has chosen to cut up like stone? But Aristotle and Plato and Empedocles and Pythagoras and Democritus and all those who have given heed to understanding the truth about these animals have perceived that they have a share of reason (*logou*).

(De abstinentia [On Abstinence from Animal Flesh] III. 6. 5–6)

Just about everybody believes that, with respect to perception (*aisthēseōs*) and the rest of our organization that pertains to the senses and the flesh, we are set up in the same way [as are animals]. For they share with us not only natural experiences and the movements that these experiences inspire, but also unnatural diseased experiences that are observable in them. No reasonable person would assert that, because of differences in the constitution of their bodies, they are incapable of a rational disposition (*logikēs diatheseōs*), if he observes that in the case of human beings there is much variation of constitution according to race and nationality, while agreeing that all are equally rational.

(On Abstinence from Animal Flesh III. 7. 2)

10. Augustine

Although one does not usually think of St. Augustine (Aurelius Augustinus, 354–430 CE) as a significant contributor to the ancient debate on the nature of animalkind and on human–animal relations, he played an important role in ensuring that Stoic arguments against according reason to animals and in support of the position that humans have, in consequence of this irrationality, no obligation to refrain from using animals in any way that benefits humans, would become enshrined in Western culture through the influence of the Church. Rational beings (that is, humans), through the possession of reason, approximate God, in Augustine's view, while irrational animals cannot hope to approximate God (*Confessions* VII. 17). The task of animals is to aid humans along their journey to salvation. This is not to say that animals are not without their own beauty and excellences, since, after all, as Romans 1:20 reminds the believer, one recognizes God through the things that he has made.

In the passage translated below, Augustine, discussing the commandment "Thou shalt not kill," answers the possible extension of the commandment to human treatment of animals by invoking the Stoic-inspired argument that God's injunction is meant to apply solely to rational beings, which leaves out not only animals but plants too. Augustine's comments are directed specifically against the sect of Manicheans, named for their founder Mani of Babylon (216–276 CE), who taught that the universe is marked by a duality of light and darkness. The forces of evil captured some of the light of the universe but by eating plants, the Manicheans believed, they could release some light into the universe again. Manichean holy-men were vegetarians, but the lower levels of adherents were permitted to consume meat if they had not themselves slain the animals. Since the Manicheans seem to have believed that plants contain more light than do animals, it is sometimes maintained that they valued plants more highly than animals that have a clearer origin in the world of darkness. Augustine appears here to have more interest in Manichean attitudes toward animals than toward plants, judging from his Stoic-inspired argument against rationality in animals, but it is interesting to note that the passage incorporates an instance of a slide argument, according to which one will be compelled to spare animals if one spares the lives of plants.

Animals Are Not Rational and Are Ours to Use

Nor it is without reason that in the holy canonical books we never find it divinely pre-scribed or permitted to us to kill ourselves, either in order to attain immortality or to avoid and escape any ill. For we must understand that we are in fact forbidden [to commit suicide], as the law says, "You shall not kill," especially since it does not add "your neighbor," as it does when it forbids false testimony, "You shall not give false testimony against your neighbor." Nor if someone has borne false testimony against himself should he suppose that he is free of this error since he who loves himself accepts the model for love of his neighbor [from love of self], as is written, "You will love your neighbor as yourself." If, then, he is no less guilty of bearing false testimony who speaks falsely against himself than if he did so against his neighbor, even if in that com-mandment in which false testimony is forbidden the prohibition is made concerning the neighbor, and it might seem to those who do not understand it that it is not forbidden to be a false witness against oneself, how much more should we understand that a man may not kill himself, since in the prescription, "You shall not kill," no additions are set forth, and in any case he to whom the prescription is made is not understood to be excepted!

Now, some attempt to extend this precept to beasts and herds as well, so that one could on this principle not kill any of them. Why not then include the plants and all that is rooted in and nourished by the earth? For this class of things, though it does not possess sensation, is said to live and can therefore die. In like manner such things can be killed if violence is applied to them. Hence the apostle, in speaking of the seeds of such things, says, "That which you sow is not quickened to live without dying," and in the psalm, "He kills their vines with hail." We do not therefore judge it a sin to pluck a branch when we hear, "You shall not kill," do we, or irrationally give assent to the errors of the Manicheans, do we? Having set aside these absurdities, then, if, when we read "You shall not kill," we do not suppose that this is meant of bushes or of irrational animals that fly, swim, or walk about and crawl, because they are not akin to us through possession of any rationality, which has not been granted to them to share in common with us, in consequence of which, by the very just ordinance of the Creator, their life and death are subject to our needs, it remains that we understand the prescription, "You shall not kill" to refer to human beings, without adding "oneself" or "another human." For he who kills himself kills nothing but a human being.

(*De civitate dei* [*The City of God*] I. 20)

Notes

1 See note 3 in Preface.
2 On the specifically Judaic contribution to Philo's thought in *De animalibus*, see Terian 46–48.

Suggestions for Further Reading

1. Alcmaeon of Croton

Dickerman, Sherwood Owen, "Some Stock Illustrations of Animal Intelligence in Greek Psychology," *TAPhA* 42 (1911) 123–130.

Dierauer, Urs, "Raison ou Instinct? Le Développement de la Zoopsychologie Antique," in Barbara Cassin and Jean-Louis Labarrière, eds, *L'Animal dans l'Antiquité* (Paris: Vrin, 1997) 5–6. Dierauer speculates in this chapter that Alcmaeon's pronouncement on the distinction between human and non-human intellect may have initiated the concept, traceable later in Aristotle, that a graduated "scale of beings" exists in which non-human animals reach no higher than the level of sensation.

——, "Das Verhältnis von Mensch und Tier im griechisch-römischen Denken," in Paul Münch and Rainer Walz, eds, *Tiere und Menschen: Geschichte und Aktualität eines prekären Verhältnisses* (Paderborn: Schöningh, 1998) 43–45.

——, *Tier und Mensch im Denken der Antike: Studien zur Tierpsychologie, Anthropologie und Ethik* (Amsterdam: Grüner, 1977) 39–43.

2. Chrysippus

Diogenes Laertius, *Lives of the Philosophers* VII. 179–202 (Life of Chrysippus).
Dierauer, "Raison ou Instinct?" 18–24.
——, "Das Verhältnis" 60–69.
——, *Tier und Mensch* 221–234.

3. Plato

Dierauer, "Raison ou Instinct?" 9–10.
——, *Tier und Mensch* 66–99.

Frère, Jean, *La Bestiaire de Platon* (Paris: Éditions Kimé, 1998). The author argues against the notion that Plato saw animals primarily as metaphors and had no interest in them as creatures of nature, and holds that Plato sought to place animals in the overall scheme of the cosmos.

Kitts, David B., "Plato on Kinds of Animals," *Biology and Philosophy* 2 (1987) 315–328.

Pinotti, Patrizia, "Gli Animali in Platone: Metafore e Tassonomie," in Silvana Castignone and Giuliana Lanata, eds, *Filosofi e Animali nel Mondo Antico* (Pisa: Edizioni ETS, 1994) 101–121. Pinotti holds that Plato had little interest in animals as living creatures, but found them useful as metaphors for human virtues and vices.

4. Aristotle

Deirauer, "Raison ou Instinct?" 11–17.

——, *Tier und Mensch* 100–161.

——, "Verhältnis" 51–59.

Dumont, Jacques, *Les Animaux dans l'Antiquité* (Paris: l'Harmattan, 2001) 216–264.

Fortenbaugh, William D., "Aristotle: Animals, Emotion and Moral Virtue," *Arethusa* 4 (1972) 137–165. Fortenbaugh examines apparent contradictions in Aristotle's pronouncements on intellectual and moral qualities in animals between his ethical treatises and his biological treatises.

French, Roger, *Ancient Natural History: Histories of Nature* (London and New York: Routledge, 1994) 6–82.

Labarrière, Jean-Louis, "De la Phronesis Animale," in Daniel Devereux and Pierre Pellegrin, eds, *Biologie, Logique et Métaphysique chez Aristote* (Paris: Éditions du Centre National de la Recherche Scientifique, 1990) 405–428. The author analyzes the meanings and degrees of intellect in animals that Aristotle's use of the term *phronēsis* entails.

Pratt, Vernon, "The Essence of Aristotle's Zoology," *Phronesis* 29 (1984) 267–278. Pratt argues that Aristotle's main interest in biology was not in classifying animals but in understanding why they have the characteristics that they possess by nature.

Preus, Anthony, "Animal and Human Souls in the Peripatetic School," *Skepsis* 1 (1990) 67–99.

——, *Science and Philosophy in Aristotle's Biological Works* (Hildesheim: Olms, 1975). The work contains useful information on Aristotle's role as an observational biologist.

Renehan, Robert, "The Greek Anthropocentric View of Man," *HSCPh* 85 (1981) 239–259. Renehan offers a helpful introduction, with extensive citations from classical texts, to the idea, frequently voiced in Aristotle, that man alone of animals possesses particular talents and skills, a notion that Renehan considers a manifestation of a strong current of anthropocentrism in classical thought on animals.

Solmsen, Friedrich, "Antecedents of Aristotle's Psychology and Scale of Beings," *AJPh* 76 (1955) 148–164. Solmsen notes some anticipations of the idea of a scale of beings in Plato, who understood the idea in an ethical rather than in a biological sense.

Sorabji, Richard, *Animal Minds and Human Morals: The Origins of the Western Debate* (Ithaca: Cornell University Press, 1993). This study traces the ramifications, in subsequent thought into the present day, of Aristotle's denial of reason to non-human animals.

Vegetti, Mario, "Figure dell' Animale in Aristotele," in Castignone and Lanata, eds, *Filosofi e Animale nel Mondo Antico* 123–137. Vegetti maintains that Aristotle's influence on later biology encouraged a fascination with taxonomy to the detriment of actual observation of animal species.

5. Philo of Alexandria

Dickerman, "Some Stock Illustrations of Animal Intelligence."

Mühl, Max, "Der λόγος ἐνδιάθετος und προφορικός von der älteren Stoa bis zur Synode von Sirmium 351," *Archiv für Begriffsgeschichte* 7 (1962) 7–56.

Newmyer, Stephen T., "Philo on Animal Psychology: Sources and Moral Implications," in Samuel Kottek and Manfred Horstmanshoff, eds, *From Athens to Jerusalem: Medicine in Ancient Jewish and Early Christian Literature* (Rotterdam: Erasmus Publishing, 2000) 143–155. This study examines Philo's use of Stoic ideas in his case against animal rationality.

Renehan, Robert, "The Greek Anthropocentric View of Man."

Terian, Abraham, *Philonis Alexandrini de Animalibus: The Armenian Text with an Introduction, Translation and Commentary* (Chico, CA: Scholars Press, 1981).

6. Seneca

Dierauer, *Tier und Mensch* 199–245.

——, "Das Verhältnis" 60–69.

7. Plutarch

d'Agostino, Vittorio, "Sulla Zoopsicologia di Plutarco," *Arch. Ital. di Psicologia* 11 (1933) 21–42. This early study examines Plutarch's critique of the views of various ancient schools of philosophy on the psychology of animals and offers interesting comments on Plutarch's anticipations of "modern" attitudes toward animal intellect.

Barigazzi, Adelmo, "Implicanze Morali nella Polemica Plutarchea sulla Psicologia degli Animali," in Italo Gallo, ed., *Plutarco e le Scienze* (Genoa: Sagep Editrice, 1992) 297–315.

Becchi, Francesco, "Istinto e Intelligenza negli Scritti Zoopsicologici di Plutarco," in Michele Bandini and Federico G. Pericoli, eds, *Scritti in Memoria di Dino Pieraccioni* (Florence: Istituto Papirologico G. Vitelli, 1993) 59–83. Becchi discusses the ancient philosophical schools to which Plutarch seems to be indebted in his animal treatises.

Bréchet, Christophe, "La Philosophie de Gryllos," in Jacques Boulogne, ed., *Les Grecs et les Animaux: Le Cas Remarquable de Plutarque* (Lille: Collection UL3, 2005) 43–61. Bréchet argues that the influence of Plato on the philosophy of Gryllus has been underestimated and that Gryllus' point is that animals are superior to humans because in them the three elements of the Platonic soul are in harmony, in contrast to the situation in human beings.

Dickerman, "Some Stock Illustrations of Animal Intelligence."

Dierauer, *Tier und Mensch* 186–193, 279–293.

Newmyer, Stephen T., *Animals, Rights and Reason in Plutarch and Modern Ethics* (Oxford: Routledge, 2006). This volume offers an overview of Plutarch's philosophy on animals and their place in the scheme of human morality, with discussion of Plutarch's anticipations of arguments raised in modern animal rights literature.

Santese, Giuseppina, "Animali e Razionalità in Plutarco," in S. Castignone and G. Lanata, eds, *Filosofi e Animali nel Mondo Antico* 141–170. Santese traces Plutarch's debt to various ancient schools of philosophy and attempts to reconcile apparent contradictions in his assertions on animals.

8. Aelian

French, *Ancient Natural History: Histories of Nature* 260–276.

9. Porphyry

Clark, Gillian, trans., *Porphyry: On Abstinence from Killing Animals* (Ithaca: Cornell University Press, 2000). The Introduction to Clark's translation of Porphyry's treatise provides much useful background material on Porphyry and his writings, as well as on many aspects of his approach to the topic of philosophical vegetarianism.

Dierauer, *Tier und Mensch* 80–89, 170–177.

Dombrowski, Daniel A., *The Philosophy of Vegetarianism* (Amherst: University of Massachusetts Press, 1984). The work contains a helpful summary of the contents of Porphyry's treatise.

Haussleiter, Johannes, *Der Vegetarismus in der Antike* (Berlin: Töpelmann, 1935) 316–337.

Pérez-Paoli, Ubaldo, "Porphyrios' Gedanken zur Gerechtigkeit gegenüber den Tieren," in Friedrich Niewöhner and Jean-Loup Sebon, eds, *Die Seele der Tiere* (Wiesbaden: Harassowitz Verlag, 2001) 93–110. The author maintains that Porphyry's position on justice toward animals rests on the likeness that reason bears to the divine.

Preus, Anthony, "Biological Theory in Porphyry's *De abstinentia*," *Ancient Philosophy* 3 (1983) 149–159. Preus examines Porphyry's ecological arguments, including his belief that animals will self-regulate their numbers and contribute naturally to the balance of nature if left alone.

10. Augustine

Gilhus, Ingvild, *Animals, Gods and Humans: Changing Attitudes to Animals in Greek, Roman and Early Christian Ideas* (Oxford: Routledge, 2006) 258–260. Gilhus offers a detailed discussion of the place of plants and animals in the Manichean scheme of the universe.

Sorabji, *Animal Minds and Human Morals* 102–113, 195–198.

2

HUMAN–ANIMAL KINSHIP

1. Aristotle

The passage that follows appears not long after Aristotle's notorious and lamentably influential assertions in the *Politics* that human slaves are living pieces of property and that slavery is a natural phenomenon since one group must necessarily rule over another. Just as it is natural for one man to rule over another, so it is natural for humans to rule over animals, for they are intended for man's use in the same way that some humans are intended for the use of other humans. In this starkly anthropocentric passage, we glimpse, at least by implication, both Aristotle's concept of teleology, whereby all things are designed toward some end, and his doctrine of *sunecheia*, or biological gradualism, according to which nature moves gradually from lower beings to higher beings, although the subtlety with which Aristotle understands that doctrine is absent from our passage. Our excerpt appears immediately before another famous and influential Aristotelian assertion in the *Politics*, namely that when unruly groups of human beings or animals that are naturally meant to be ruled by others refuse to submit to control, their superiors may conduct a "just war" against them. The concept of "just war" has been used throughout history to justify actions ranging from the hunting of animals to the subjugation and colonization of entire societies.

Animals Are Created for Man's Use

Thus we must suppose that nature [cares for] animals in like manner when they are once alive, and that plants exist for the sake of animals and the other animals for the sake of men, domesticated animals for both his use and his food and most of the wild ones, if not all, for his food and other needs, so that clothing and other products might be produced from them. If then nature makes nothing without purpose or at random, it is necessary that nature has produced all these things for the sake of man.

(*Politics* 1256b15–23)

2. Diogenes Laertius

The following passage from Diogenes Laertius' biography of Zeno (335–263 BCE), the founder of Stoicism, is the classic exposition of the nature of the concept termed *oikeiōsis*. Notoriously difficult to define, the term has variously been interpreted as the recognition of kinship, relationship or belonging that is perceived to exist between individuals following a prior recognition by an individual of his own self and of what belongs to him and is appropriate to himself and of what is alien and foreign to him. According to Stoic teaching, a human being moves from the stage in which he recognizes only himself and his own wants and needs to a recognition of his kinship with others at that time at which reason becomes operational in him which occurs at either seven or fourteen years of age, depending on the Stoic source expounding the doctrine.

The noun *oikeiōsis* is derived from the noun *oikia*, "house, household," and naturally contains connotations of belonging and association and, by implication, of not belonging and alienation. Some scholars have argued that the concept can be traced already to the works of Aristotle's follower Theophrastus (*c*.370–287 BCE) who argued, apparently in his work *On Piety*, that animal sacrifice is wrong because animals and human beings share a kinship based on some intellectual similarities, so that a relationship of justice exists between humans and other animal species. The Stoics countered that rational human beings have no intellectual kinship with irrational animals, so that no kinship can be said to exist between species and no debt of justice is possible between species.

The Stoic Theory of "Kinship" (*oikeiōsis*)

They say that the animal directs its first impulse toward self-preservation because nature from the very beginning endears (*oikeiousēs*) a thing to itself, according to what Chrysippus says in the first book of his *On Ends*. He declares, "The thing which first and foremost belongs (*oikeion einai*) to every animal is its own constitution and its consciousness of that." For it is not reasonable that nature would estrange (*allotriōsai*) an animal from itself or, after making a creature, would cause it to be either alien to or not akin to itself. Therefore, we are left to conclude that nature, in putting a creature together, has caused it to be attracted to its own self, for thus it flees those things that are alien to itself and pursues those things that are akin to itself.

(*Lives of the Philosophers* **VII**. 85 [from the life of Zeno the Stoic])

3. Epicurus

Epicureanism is not a philosophical system that one generally associates with ancient discussion on the nature of animalkind or on the relationship, biological and ethical, between human and non-human animals. The extant fragments of the writings of Epicurus (341–270 BCE), most of which are found in the tenth book of Diogenes Laertius' *Lives of the Philosophers*, scarcely mention animals, but two of the so-called *Sovereign Maxims*, which are found at the end of Diogenes' life of Epicurus, do speculate on the question of whether human beings can stand in any relationship of justice with animals. The forty *Maxims*, short and pithy formulations of key points in Epicurean doctrine, may have been intended for memorization by the followers of the Master. Maxims 31–32, translated below, maintain that justice and injustice are impossible between humans and non-human animals, or between one non-human animal species and another, because animals are incapable of forming contracts or covenants setting forth their intention to respect each other's interests. Such an agreement, in Epicurean teaching, requires language and Epicurus denied the capacity for meaningful language to non-human species. The idea that justice arises from a contract between individuals to respect the rights of others and to assert a desire that one's own rights be respected in like measure, lives on in the modern ethical stance variously termed Contractualism, Contractarianism, and Contract Theory. Although ancient precedents for contract ethics are more highly developed in Stoicism (see below, p. 60), the presuppositions of the position are traceable as well in the *Maxims* of Epicurus.

Justice Is a Matter of Forming Covenants

Justice by nature is a covenant arising from expediency, whereby [persons agree] not to harm each other and not to be harmed. There is no justice or injustice in relation to animals that are not capable of forming contracts (*sunthēkās*) not to harm one another and not to be harmed. Such races as could not or did not wish to form contracts not to cause harm or be harmed are similar.

(*Kuriai Doxai [Sovereign Maxims]* XXXI and XXXII of Epicurus as cited in Diogenes Laertius, *Lives of the Philosophers* X. 150 [from the life of Epicurus])

4. Lucretius

The Roman Epicurean philosopher–poet Titus Lucretius Carus (*c*.94–55 BCE) is our best source of information on the Epicurean philosophical system beyond the relatively meager fragments from Epicurus himself that are contained in Diogenes Laertius' biography of the Master (*Lives of the Philosophers* X). His didactic poem *De rerum natura* (*On the Nature of Things*), in six books, provides a detailed exposition of the atomistic view of the universe that Epicurus taught. Although Epicurean physics is treated at length and systematically, ethical aspects of the system are only incidentally touched upon, which has led some to speculate that the poem survives in an incomplete state.

Epicurus did not encourage innovation in the system's teachings on the part of his disciples, and it is usually maintained that, because Lucretius was a passionate and convinced adherent of the Epicurean school, he did not offer any innovations himself. The passage translated below, derived from the poet's account of the rise of human civilization contained in the fifth book of *On the Nature of Things*, seems to contradict this assertion. The poet here explains how some species of animals joined with human beings to benefit from human guardianship (*tutela*) in return for which they offered humans their services and products. Lucretius appears to suggest that covenants or contracts are after all possible between animal species, despite Epicurus' assertions to the contrary. The arrangement proved beneficial to humans and non-human species alike both in providing some sense of stability and in fostering the growth of agriculture and animal domestication. Lucretius' vision of interspecies contract formation lacks the subtlety of Epicurus' formulation in his *Sovereign Maxims* since the Roman poet does not specifically connect this relationship with the growth of justice and he does not hint at language possession as a prerequisite for contract formation, but it is interesting to note that Lucretius, here and elsewhere in *On the Nature of Things*, has a more affectionate and appreciative view of non-human animals than did his master Epicurus.

Covenants Are Possible between Humans and Animals

Many generations of animals necessarily perished then and were unable to establish their progeny by reproduction. For those animals that you observe breathing life-giving air were preserved by cleverness or strength or perhaps speed since the beginning of time. And there are many species which were entrusted to our care because of their usefulness to us. In the first instance, strength preserved the fierce race of lions, while cleverness preserved foxes and speed preserved deer. But the light-sleeping breeds of dogs, with their faithful hearts, and every species of draft animals and likewise fleecy sheep and the generations of horned beasts: all these, Memmius, have been entrusted to our guardianship (*tutelae*), for they have happily escaped wild beasts and have pursued peace along with plentiful food secured without any effort on their part, which we gave to them as a reward for their helpfulness to us. But those species on which nature bestowed none of these qualities and which could neither live on their own nor supply us with any useful service, in return for which we would allow them to feed under our protection and remain safe, those species of course lay victim to others, all bound by their own fatal chains until nature relegated those species to destruction.

(De rerum natura [On the Nature of Things] V. 855–877)

5. Philo of Alexandria

In this final paragraph from his treatise *De animalibus* (*On Animals*), Philo combines the two intellectual traditions that inspired his treatise – Judaism and Stoicism. It is noteworthy that Philo very seldom relies on arguments of a religious nature in opposing his nephew Alexander's claims of rationality in animals, depending rather on Stoic-inspired denials of interspecies kinship, the *oikeiōsis* of the Stoics. In these final sentences, however, Philo suggests that to claim that animals are rational insults God and the special position in the scheme of creation that God has accorded to human beings.

Animal Have No Kinship with Humans

Let us now stop criticizing nature and committing sacrilege. To elevate animals to the level of the human race and to grant equality to unequals is the height of injustice. To ascribe serious self-restraint to indifferent and almost invisible creatures is to insult those whom nature has endowed with the best part.

(On Animals 100)

6. Pliny the Elder

Gaius Plinius Secundus (23–79 CE), called the Elder to distinguish him from his similarly named nephew, is the compiler of a thirty-seven volume encyclopedia called *Naturalis Historia* (*Natural History*), a work that he himself claims contains material drawn from 2000 written sources. A valuable and fascinating depository of facts (and fictions) on subjects as far-reaching as agriculture, metallurgy, botany and art history, Pliny's work includes four books (VIII–XI) on zoological topics, although animals are discussed in various contexts throughout the work, in particular in books XXVIII–XXXII on pharmaceuticals derived from animal products. While it would be a gross exaggeration to call Pliny a naturalist in the manner of Aristotle or Theophrastus, it is nevertheless possible to divine some view of the place of animals in the scheme of creation embedded in his innumerable accounts of miraculous deeds and characteristics of animals. He agreed with Aristotle that animals were intended by nature to serve man's needs, but he abhorred mistreatment of animals by humans. He denied reason to animals but he frequently recounted anecdotes in which animals are shown to have behaviors analogous to those of humans. In the excerpt that follows, he suggests that some animals have religious sensibilities because certain species demonstrate behaviors that resemble those of humans at worship. He contradicts a number of ancient assertions that only man has religious sensibilities (for example, Xenophon, *Memorabilia* I. 4. 13; Plato, *Protagoras* 322a; Cicero, *Laws* I. 8. 24). Pliny's formulation of the issue leaves him open to the charge of anthropomorphization that is frequently leveled against modern ethologists – specialists in animal behavior, who seek to suggest that animals have moral qualities evident in human beings.

Similarities between Humans and Animals

Let us pass to the remaining animals, and first to the land-dwellers. The elephant is the largest and the closest to humans in intelligence (*sensibus*). Indeed, [it demonstrates] understanding of the language used in its homeland, obedience to orders, recollection of what is has learned, pleasure in affection and fame, goodness, discretion and fairness (which are rare even in a human being), as well as reverence for the stars and veneration of the sun and moon. Authorities report that in the woodlands of Mauretania, herds of them come to a particular river whose name is Amilo at the time when the new moon is bright, and, purifying themselves, they sprinkle themselves with water and thus, after greeting the moon, they return to the forests, carrying their weary calves in front of them. They are believed, due to their understanding of the religious scruples of others, to be unwilling to climb on board ships when they are about to cross the seas until they have been enticed by the oath of their masters promising their return. They have been observed, when weary from sickness (illnesses beset even those with huge bodies) to lie on their backs and toss grasses to heaven, as if the earth were bound by their entreaties. As far as concerns their docility, they reverence their king by bending their knee and offering him garlands. The smaller ones, which they call the bastard elephant, are employed by the Indians for ploughing.

(*Natural History* VIII. 1)

7. Plutarch

In his dialogue *De sollertia animalium* (*On the Cleverness of Animals*), Plutarch's inter-locutors Aristotimus and Phaedimus debate the relative degree of "cleverness" exhibited by land-dwelling and sea-dwelling animals, with Aristotimus maintain-ing the intellectual superiority of land-dwellers and Phaedimus that of sea-dwellers. Ultimately, neither side proves victorious in the debate as all animals are declared to possess "cleverness." In the passage from *On the Cleverness of Animals* translated below, Phaedimus, at the outset of his comments, argues that it is much more difficult to make a case for the cleverness of sea-dwelling species because they are so seldom observable to the human eye and consequently seem alien to human beings, while land-dwelling species are likely to strike humans as more like them because of their physical proximity to humans which serves to render them more "akin" to humans in manners and lifestyle through an imitation of human habits. In so arguing, Phaedimus makes an oblique allusion to the doctrine of *oikeiōsis*, "kinship, belonging," which Plutarch, in contrast to the Stoics, believed to exist between human and non-human animals, both land- and sea-dwellers. Plutarch ends the passage by stressing that any lack of "kinship" between humans and sea-dwelling species is only apparent and is occasioned solely by their marine existence and not by their nature itself.

The treatise *De Stoicorum repugnantiis* (*On the Self-Contradictions of the Stoics*) seeks to point out absurdities in the philosophical system of Stoicism, and in the work, Plutarch repeatedly singles out the influential early Stoic Chrysippus (see pp. 3–4) for censure. Here he notes the prominent place that the doctrine of *oikeiōsis* had in the writings of Chrysippus. Plutarch's elucidation of the Chrysippean under-standing of the doctrine demonstrates that, in Stoic parlance, such kinship existed between human and human and between animal and animal but not between human and animal. Plutarch's case for a debt of justice toward non-human ani-mals on the part of human beings set forth in *On the Cleverness of Animals* depends in part upon a demonstration of interspecies kinship based on intellectual "kinship."

Land-Dwelling Animals Are Most Akin to Humans

PHAEDIMUS: And yet there is nothing to stand in the way of [our taking] examples from land animals, since the land lies completely open to study by the senses. But the sea allows just a few stingy glimpses, and covers over the births, rearing, attacks and defenses of most of her inhabitants, among which not a few examples of understand-ing (*suneseōs*) and memory and fellowship are hidden and hinder our argument. Also, land animals, because of the relatedness of their nature [to that of human beings] and their closeness of habitation, somehow benefit from their upbringing and teaching and imitation, by virtue of their contact with human customs. This contact sweetens all their bitterness and gloominess, as river water sweetens seawater, and all their dense-ness of understanding and dullness are invigorated by interaction with humans. But the life of sea-dwellers, because it is removed from intercourse with humans by great boundaries and is alien and in no way akin to human life, is distinct and indigenous and unrelated and unmixed with customs alien to it because of location and not because of nature.

(*On the Cleverness of Animals* 975E–F)

Chrysippus Defines the Stoic Theory of "Kinship" (*oikeiōsis*)

And likewise [Chrysippus] in the following words states that nothing is akin (*oikeion*) to or appropriate to the base man, "Just as nothing is foreign to the well-bred man, so is nothing akin (*oikeion*) to the base man, since the latter sort of thing (that which is akin) is a good thing while the former (that which is foreign) is bad." By Zeus, why does he, in every book about physics and ethics, bore us by writing that as soon as we are born we are akin to one another and to our bodily parts and our offspring? In the first book of his *On Justice*, he says that even beasts in like measure have such affinity to their offspring in accord with their needs, excepting fish whose embryos are self-nourishing. But there is neither sensation among those creatures to which nothing is sensible nor kinship (*oikeiōsis*) among those to which nothing is akin, since kinship seems to be the apprehension of that which is akin.

(*De Stoicorum repugnantiis* [*On the Self-Contradictions of the Stoics*] 1038B)

8. Porphyry

The third book of Porphyry's lengthy treatise *De abstinentia* (*On Abstinence from Animal Flesh*) is given over to an elaborate defense of the position that human beings owe a debt of justice to non-human animals, both because animals are, like humans, endowed with reason and because they understand justice and practice it in their own lives. The passage below is rich in ideas central to Porphyry's argument for justice toward animals: he alludes to the Stoic doctrine of *oikeiōsis* by chastising the absurdity of those who would admit that animals possess some degree of rationality but would still deny them any kinship with human beings, and he brings up the question of contracts (*sunthēkai*), the importance of which we have observed in the Epicurean denial of justice toward animals (see Selection 3 on pp. 28–29), arguing that we would not conclude that humans who do not form contracts with us are consequently irrational, so that, by implication, we should not conclude that animals that behave similarly are necessarily irrational. Porphyry's ingenious argument that the very presence of vices in animals proves their rationality since vice is a failure to heed reason would be rejected by the Stoics who held that animals cannot choose to be either virtuous or vicious because they cannot live their lives in accord with reason in the first place.

Animals Are Akin to Humans because They Are Rational

But someone might say that [animals] are rational but do not possess any relationship to us. Yet it was because of their being irrational that they removed their relationship to us. They make them irrational since they … And there is the [position] of those who derive our association with animals from need, not from reason. But we proposed to show whether they are rational, not whether they form covenants (*sunthekās*) with us.

No one would say that, because not every man forms a covenant with us, he who does not is therefore irrational. And yet most animals are slaves to human beings and, as someone rightly said, although they are enslaved from the ignorance of human beings, still, because of their wisdom (*sophiās*) and justice (*dikaiosunēs*), they have made their masters into their underlings and caretakers. Their vices are obvious, in consequence of which their rationality is revealed most clearly, for they exhibit jealousy and rivalries over females, just as the females do over the males. But the one vice that they do not exhibit is treachery toward someone of goodwill, but they demonstrate goodwill in each instance themselves. They have so little fear of a person of goodwill that they follow him even if he leads them to slaughter and manifest danger. And too they feel goodwill toward their owner even if he feeds them not for their own sake but rather out of his own interests. But humans conspire against no one so much as against him who nourishes them, and they pray for no one's death so much as for his.

(*On Abstinence from Animal Flesh III*. 13. 1–3)

Suggestions for Further Reading

1. Aristotle

Dierauer, *Tier und Mensch* 155–157.

Sorabji 134–138. Sorabji offers a discussion of the part played by *Politics* 1256b13–26 and related Aristotelian texts in the debate concerning the colonization of the New World by Spain and in the treatment of New World populations following their subjugation by Europeans.

2. Diogenes Laertius

Becchi, Francesco, "Biopsicologia e Giustizia verso gli Animali in Teofrasto e Plutarco," *Prometheus* 27 (2001) 119–135. This study maintains that Plutarch employed material from Theophrastus to argue that one can be both just and pious toward animals.

Brink, C.O.,"Οἰκείωσις and Οἰκειότης: Theophrastus and Zeno on Moral Theory," *Phronesis* 1 (1955–56) 123–145. Brink considers the Theophrastean contribution to *oikeiōsis* theory to be exaggerated and the importance of the idea to Stoic ethics to be overstated by scholars.

Dirlmeier, Franz, "Die Oikeiosis-Lehre Theophrasts," *Philologus Supplementband* 30 (1937) 1–100. This is the most influential argument for Theophrastean influence on the development of subsequent *oikeiōsis* theory.

Obbink, Dirk, "The Origin of Greek Sacrifice: Theophrastus on Religion and Cultural History," in William W. Fortenbaugh and Robert W. Sharples, eds, *Theophrastean Studies on Natural Science, Physics and Metaphysics, Ethics, Religion, and Rhetoric* (New Brunswick: Transaction Books, 1988) 272–295. Obbink speculates on the structure of Theophrastus' lost treatise *On Piety*, and declares it valuable as a Peripatetic vision of the doctrine of *oikeiōsis*.

Pembroke, S.G., "Oikeiōsis," in A.A. Long, ed., *Problems in Stoicism* (London: Athlone Press, 1971) 114–149. This chapter offers valuable discussion of the etymology of the term *oikeiōsis*.

Striker, Gisela, "The Role of *Oikeiosis* in Stoic Ethics," *OSAPh* 1 (1983) 145–167. Striker discusses the connection of the concept of *oikeiōsis* with Stoic notions of the origins of justice.

3. Epicurus

DeLacy, Phillip, "The Epicurean Analysis of Language," *AJPh* 60 (1939) 85–92. DeLacy argues that the Epicureans took a practical view of language as a tool arising from convention and necessity, and that they scorned poetic and metaphorical language as unscientific and useless.

Dierauer, *Tier und Mensch* 194–198.

Gauthier, David P., *Morals by Agreement* (Oxford: Clarendon Press, 1986). This volume sets forth a modern ethical system based on contract theory.

Huby, Pamela M., "The Epicureans, Animals, and Freewill," *Apeiron* 3 (1969) 17–19. Huby demonstrates that the Epicureans seem to have accorded freewill to humans but not to animals.

Mitsis, Phillip, *Epicurus' Ethical Theory: The Pleasures of Invulnerability* (Ithaca: Cornell, 1988). Mitsis offers an extended discussion of the part played by contract forming in Epicurean ethics, although without specific reference to animals.

4. Lucretius

Budiansky, Stephen, *The Covenant of the Wild: Why Animals Choose Domestication* (New York: William Morrow, 1992). Budiansky develops at length the position advanced in the fifth book of Lucretius that domestication of animals happened naturally in a manner that benefitted human and non-human species by providing both with useful services and protecting both from danger and want.

Shelton, Jo-Ann, "Contracts with Animals: Lucretius, De Rerum Natura," *Between the Species* 11 (1995) 115–121. Shelton argues that the interspecies contract formation that Lucretius envisions helped humans to achieve the pleasure that is the goal of the Epicurean system by reducing anxiety among humans who were provided with services that bettered human life.

———, "Lucretius on the Use and Abuse of Animals," *Eranos* 94 (1996) 48–64. This article maintains that human beings produce for themselves the pleasure that Epicureans coveted by being willing to fulfill obligations toward some animals while secluding themselves from other animal species.

5. Philo of Alexandria

Newmyer, "Philo on Animal Psychology: Sources and Implications." This study touches upon ways in which Philo manages to incorporate articles of Jewish faith into the Stoic-influenced dialogue *On Animals*.

Terian, Abraham, "A Critical Introduction to Philo's Dialogues," *ANRW* II. 21, 1 (1984) 272–294. Terian demonstrates that although Philo makes no direct use of scriptural material in *On Animals*, the anthropocentric slant of Scripture clearly influenced his assertion that to equate humans and animals is sacrilegious.

6. Pliny the Elder

Beagon, Mary, *Roman Nature: The Thought of Pliny the Elder* (Oxford: Clarendon Press, 1992). Beagon offers a valuable appreciation of Pliny as a philosopher of nature and attempts to formulate a coherent picture of his world view and of its animal, vegetable and mineral components.

Bodson, L., "Aspects of Pliny's Zoology," in Roger French and Frank Greenaway, eds, *Science in the Early Roman Empire: Pliny the Elder, His Sources and Influence* (Totawa, NJ: Barnes and Noble Books, 1986) 98–110. Bodson provides a summary of Pliny's sources, methods and aims as a scientist.

French, *Ancient Natural History* 196–253.

Newmyer, Stephen T., "Paws to Reflect: Ancients and Moderns on the Religious Sensibilities of Animals," *QUCC* 75, 3 (2003) 111–129. This study surveys the debate on whether animals have religious feelings and how these are manifested in animals, according to ancient writers and modern ethologists.

7. *Plutarch*

Becchi, "Biopsicologia e Giustizia verso gli Animali in Teofrasto e Plutarco."

8. *Porphyry*

Pérez-Paoli, "Porphyrios' Gedanken zur Gerechtigkeit gegenüber den Tieren" 106–109. Pérez-Paoli argues that Porphyry's understanding of the Stoic concept of *oikeiōsis* was influenced by his study of Plutarch and developed in accordance with Porphyry's belief that the human person, as an image of God, seeks to avoid causing harm and strives to live in accord with reason, recognizing the rational element in animals as well as in human beings.

3

ANIMAL BEHAVIORS

1. Introductory

Plutarch

The doctrine that animals are superior to human beings, which is sometimes termed animalitarianism or "theriophily" ("love of beasts"), entails an admiration for the character and behavior of non-human species vis-à-vis those of humans and may have originated in classical thought in a reaction to Aristotle's assertion that humans alone are rational and are consequently elevated above the rest of animal creation. Other sources may include the Cynics who professed to admire the demeanor of animals that lived, unlike humans, close to nature (*phusis*) and avoided the artifices that plagued human life. At times, the position included the assertion that non-human species were rational, like their human counterparts, and at others that non-human species were better off in a non-rational state since they were not led astray by a clever and scheming intellect. Because theriophilic assertions often appear in contexts in which human behavior is being censured, it is often difficult to determine whether the admiration for animals is seriously intended or satirically employed. In any case, there are few extant instances of this strain of thought in classical literature, and none so elaborately developed as the account of animal excellences contained in Plutarch's treatise *Bruta animalia ratione uti* (*Whether Beasts Are Rational*), wherein the philosophical pig Gryllus lectures Odysseus on the moral failings of human beings. One may conclude that Plutarch's assumption of a strongly theriophilic stance here is largely satirical since the doctrine is otherwise absent from Plutarch's animal treatises, however admiring he may elsewhere show himself to be of the intellectual attainments of animals.

Are Animals in Fact Superior to Human Beings?

GRYLLUS: Now you are allowing that the soul of a beast is more naturally disposed and more perfectly arranged toward the production of virtue, for without command or training, and, so to speak, uncultivated and unploughed, it brings forth and causes to flourish the virtue proper to each sort of animal.

ODYSSEUS: And of which virtue, dear Gryllus, do animals have a share?

GRYLLUS: Of which do they not have a share, to a degree greater than do humans! Look at their courage, a virtue in which you take such great pride and about which you do not blush when called "bold" and "sacker of cities." But you, O miserable fellow, by your tricks and schemes misled men who knew only a simple and noble manner of war-making and who were without experience of deceit and lies, and you placed on your knavery the name of that virtue which is least suited to that misbehavior. Yet you see how guilelessly and artlessly animals carry out their battles against one another and against us, with true naked courage and genuine valor. An unconquerable will to prevail to the end strengthens and sustains them that fear no summons or indictment for desertion, for they are not defeated even when conquered in body, nor do they surrender in spirit but die fighting. In the case of many animals at the point of death, their valor withdraws along with their high spirits and gathers itself up into one point in their bodies, and it resists the creature that kills it, leaping about and raging, until, like a fire, it is entirely extinguished and dies. There is no entreaty or begging for mercy or acknowledgement of defeat, nor does one lion become the slave of another or a horse to a horse, as does one man to another when he calmly welcomes the name of slave that is derived from the word "cowardice." And of those beasts which humans have mastered with snares and tricks, those that are full-grown push away food and bear up against thirst and welcome and greet death sooner than slavery. In the case of nestlings and whelps, however, that are easily led and gentle because of their youth, humans offer them many alluring treats and beguilements, intoxicating them, and in time they make them partial to pleasures that are contrary to their nature and enfeeble them, until they accept and endure the so-called taming that is actually an effeminization of their spirit. In light of these facts, it is clear that animals are born with a predisposition toward courage, whereas in humans, an enduring spirit is contrary to nature.

(Whether Beasts Are Rational 987B–F)

Aelian

In the opening paragraph of his seventeen-book compilation of animal wonders, which are assembled more for their ability to astonish the reader than for their scientific probability, Aelian reveals a genuine enthusiasm for nature's marvels if no deep appreciation for its workings. In the short compass of his Prologue, he alludes to a number of issues and concepts central to Greco-Roman speculation on the nature of animalkind and on the comparative excellences of human and non-human animals, including man's unique possession of reason and its relation to speech, likewise uniquely human, and the admission that in some instances, animals are endowed with excellent properties that humans lack. Aelian freely acknowledges the limitations of his work, especially its lack of scientific and philosophical depth when set against the work of his predecessors, but he boasts that his treatise has at least the virtues of clarity and elegance of expression. Aelian's pride in his stylistic excellence is a reflection of the fact that he was of Italian birth and learned Greek as a second language, beginning his career as a sophistical declaimer before taking up literary composition.

Introduction on the Characteristics of Animals

Perhaps it is not to be wondered at if man is wise and just and very careful concerning his own children, and if he demonstrates a fitting regard for his parents, and if he seeks after food for himself, is on guard against plots, and has all the other gifts of nature that he possesses. For man has been accorded speech, the most prized of all possessions, and has been granted reason, which is the most helpful and serviceable endowment. And too he knows how to reverence and worship the gods. But the fact that irrational animals share some degree of excellence and possess many of mankind's advantages and wonders that are assigned to him, is a great thing too. To know readily the characteristics that are possessed by each, and to appreciate how the characteristics of other animals are a matter of no less serious interest than are those of human beings, would be the task of a well-trained mind endowed with much knowledge. I know full well how much effort has been expended on this subject by others, but I have collected all such material as I was able and have dressed it in common language, and I am convinced that I have produced a treasure of no small merit. If this collection seems useful to anyone, let him use it, while he to whom it does not seem so should give it to his father to cherish and care for. Not all things are valuable to all persons, and not all are eager to pursue the same subjects. If I was born after many earlier wise men, let that fact of my birthdate not damage my reputation, if I have produced a work worthy of serious consideration, both on account of its rather elaborate conception and of its style.

(*On the Nature of Animals*, Prologue)

Suggestions for Further Reading

Plutarch

Boas, George, "Theriophily," in Philip P. Wiener, ed., *Dictionary of the History of Ideas* (New York: Scribners, 1973), IV, 384–389.

Dierauer, *Tier und Mensch* 180–193.

Gill, James E., "Theriophily in Antiquity: A Supplementary Account," *JHI* 30 (1969) 401–412.

Lovejoy, Arthur O. and George Boas, *Primitivism and Related Ideas in Antiquity* (Baltimore: Johns Hopkins University Press, 1935). Chapter XIII, "The Superiority of the Animals," 389–420, gives a historical survey of manifestations of theriophilic thought in Greek and Roman sources from Xenophon through Plutarch.

Aelian

French, *Ancient Natural History: Histories of Nature* 260–276.

2. Rearing of Offspring

Homer

Although Homer (8th century BCE?) lived long before the earliest stages of Greek biological investigation, the two epic poems attributed to him, the *Iliad* and the *Odyssey*, are replete with references to animals. Scholars have isolated the names of approximately one hundred types of animals in Homer, although some cannot be identified with certainty. With notable exceptions, Homeric references to animals appear in the context of poetic similes in which the poet likens human activities and behavior to those of animals that are singled out for bravery, industriousness, sloth, steadfastness, and a host of other virtues and vices observable in his heroes. Although one would search in vain for any attempt at systematic classification of animals in the Homeric corpus, it is well to remember in any case that Homer lived in a society that had closer contact with animals than did the Greeks of Aristotle's time and that the poet's observations may reflect some degree of eye-witness familiarity.

Considerable attention has been paid to Homeric vocabulary relating to the physical and intellectual make-up of animals. It is noteworthy that Homer does not employ the word *zōion* that is regularly used in Greek for "animal," and he uses the term *thūmos* to refer to the animal soul, in preference to the word *psuchē* usually used of the human soul.

Homer seems to have had a certain tenderness toward animals and a sympathy for their hardships, observable, for example, in Patroclus' touching account (*Iliad* V. 192–203) of how he left his beloved horses at home in Greece rather than subject them to possible privations in battle, and especially in the poet's account of the mistreatment of Odysseus' old dog Argus during his master's absence at Troy (*Odyssey* XVII. 290–323) (see pp. 113–114). Achilles' description of how a mother bird deprives herself of food so that her young ones can eat would become a commonplace example of animal behavior in later Greek literature.

Animal Parenting in the Homeric Simile

[ACHILLES:] "But I will speak to you as seems best to me. I do not think that Agamemnon the son of Atreus or the other Danaans will persuade me since there was no gratitude for my incessant fighting against our enemies. The same fate befalls the man who holds back as the one who fights fiercely. One's honor is the same, be he coward or stalwart. The idle man dies as surely as the man who has accomplished much. I accomplish nothing by always risking my life since I suffer pain in my heart. Just as a bird brings home morsels of food for her fledgling young, when she finds it, though she is herself sorely afflicted, so have I lain awake many nights and so did I fight bloody days, battling warriors for the sake of other men's womenfolk."

(*Iliad* IX. 314–327)

Cicero

The Roman orator Marcus Tullius Cicero (106–43 BCE) used the study of Greek philosophy both to console him at the low points of his personal and political life and to occupy him in the little leisure time he enjoyed. In the latter years of his life, when he found himself increasingly marginalized with the political ascendancy of Caesar and then of his heir Octavian, later called Augustus (63 BCE–14 CE), Cicero turned to the composition of a number of philosophical treatises intended to introduce the rather unphilosophical Romans to the rich heritage of Greek philosophical thought and to provide them with a Latin philosophical vocabulary. Cicero was not an original thinker, as he freely acknowledged, terming his philosophical works mere copies (*apographa*) which he enriched with the plentiful reserve of words at his command (*Letters to Atticus* XII. 52. 3). It has been maintained that Cicero did not always grasp the intricacies of Greek thought that he attempted to express in Latin and that as a result he may at times have misrepresented the positions that he attributes to the various philosophical schools whose ideas he explicates.

Cicero's philosophical works are in most cases cast in the form of dialogues, but, like the philosophical dialogues of Plutarch and unlike those of Plato, Cicero's works are closer to essays than to true dialogues: long expositions are devoted to the views of one or another school presented by an adherent of the school whose system is being detailed. Cicero's philosophical works deal predominantly with ethical topics, while the intricacies of physics and logic interested him less.

The five books of the treatise *De finibus bonorum et malorum* (*On the Ends of Good and Evil*) set forth the position of the Stoic, Epicurean and Academic schools on the question of the highest good (*summum bonum*) in life. In the first book, Lucius Manlius Torquatus sets forth the Epicurean position that pleasure is the highest good, a view which Cicero refutes in the second book. With his deep commitment to service to the state, Cicero found the Epicurean call to pleasure and to avoidance of involvement in civic life repugnant. His reply to Torquatus suggests that he felt pleasure was unworthy of humans, although he does not take close account of the Epicurean understanding of pleasure as the absence of pain, and he suggests that pleasure be left to animals. He does in any case concede that even non-human animals at times act in ways that suggest motivations higher than mere concern for pleasure inasmuch as some animal behaviors may be motivated by the harsher and crueler aspects of animal existence. He joins writers such as Philo, Pliny the Elder and Plutarch in isolating some animals behaviors that suggest in embryonic form the commendable virtues of industry and sympathy for others of their species, not to mention traces of intellect, but he stops short of agreeing with Plutarch, who argued that the pleasures in which animals indulge, which are free of the excesses of human behavior, may serve as lessons to human beings in modest and praiseworthy conduct.

Animals Delight in Raising Their Offspring

CICERO: Therefore, Torquatus, we must discover some other highest good for human beings, and let us leave pleasure to animals, which you [Epicureans] are wont to employ as witnesses on the question of the highest good. What if even animals do many things, each incited by its own nature, that are carried out with tenderness but with struggle, as in the case of giving birth and rearing of offspring, so that it readily becomes clear that they have some other purpose than pleasure? Some animals delight in running about and wandering, while others because of their social behavior resemble the unity of a society in a certain sense. In certain species of birds we observe some indications of devotedness, recognition, recollection, and in many cases even grief for the lost.

Shall there therefore exist in beasts resemblances of human virtues that are distinct from pleasure, while in human beings themselves there will be no virtues except those carried out for the sake of pleasure? Shall we say that mankind, who far excels other creatures, has been given nothing unique by nature?

(De finibus bonorum et malorum
[On the Ends of Good and Evil] II. 109–110)

Plutarch

Plutarch's short treatise *De amore prolis* (*On the Love of Offspring*) survives in a fragmentary state, the extant portion arguing that the presence of mature rationality in human beings, which allows them to have a knowledge of justice, virtue and divinity, naturally equips them to have a richer child-rearing experience than is available to non-human species that Plutarch repeatedly calls irrational (*aloga*) in this treatise, in apparent contradiction to his position on animal rationality in *De sollertia animalium* (*On the Cleverness of Animals*). The contradiction is in fact more apparent than real since *On the Love of Offspring* is to a large extent taken up with a critique of the shortcomings of human conduct, in comparison to which animal behavior is viewed as praiseworthy and even deserving of emulation by human beings. Despite their inferior mental endowments, animals are said to live closer to nature because they do not apply such intellect as they do possess to devising ignoble actions. Ironically, Plutarch observes that it is reason itself, which he calls "autocratic" (*autokratēs logos*, *On the Love of Offspring* 494D), that leads humans to invent perverse behaviors that obliterate in humans all traces of their better nature. Consequently, humans can learn much from observing the pure and simple ways in which animals care for their offspring because their very intellectual shortcomings render it impossible for animals to teach their young the perversions that can spoil human interactions with their young. Ironically, it is animal parents that are ultimately found superior in Plutarch's account. One may detect here traces of the position, known as theriophily, according to which animals are reckoned in some particulars superior to human beings, a view that is more pronounced in Plutarch than elsewhere in classical thought on animals (see p. 37).

In the second selection below from *On the Love of Offspring*, Plutarch attacks the Epicurean idea that human parents care for their offspring strictly out of self-interest and that humans are the only animal species that is incapable of disinterested affection. Plutarch counters that it would be absurd to maintain that animals accept the pains of childbirth freely while human parents accept to profit from their offspring.

The treatise *De sollertia animalium* (*On the Cleverness of Animals*) discusses love of offspring as one source of justice in animals, both human and non-human. In that dialogue, Soclarus takes the Stoic position that animals have no understanding of justice and therefore cannot apply it in their relations with their conspecifics. Autobulus, who advances Plutarch's own views in the dialogue, detects a contradiction in the position of the Stoics, whom he calls "that group of thinkers," who are willing to acknowledge that the love of offspring is the origin of justice and, while they are willing to admit that animals have such a love in abundance, they refuse to allow that animals have any understanding of justice.

Animals Care for Their Offspring because They Live Close to Nature

Is it not also a common accusation made about human baseness, that we humans, being in doubt about the greatest and most pressing matters, seek out horses and dogs and birds [for guidance] on how we ourselves should marry and reproduce and raise offspring (as if we had no evidence of nature in us!), and that we declare the characteristics of animals to be "dispositions" and "emotions," and accuse our own life of being a great perversion from the natural and a transgression against nature, since we are from the beginning confused and mixed up concerning first principles? In animals, nature preserves what is peculiar to them in an unmixed, simple and pure form, but in human beings, under the influence of reason and habit, these traits, mingled with many opinions and additions, become, like oil in the hands of the perfumer, intricate and enticing, but do not retain their own nature. Let us not wonder if irrational animals follow nature more closely than do rational creatures, for plants do so more than do animals.

(*De amore prolis* [*On the Love of Offspring*] 493B–D)

According to Epicurus, a father loves his son, a mother loves her child, and children their parents [for pay]. But if animals should acquire understanding of speech and some one should bring to a common theater horses and cows and dogs and birds and revise this assertion and say, "Dogs do not love their pups for pay, nor horses their foals nor birds their nestlings, but they do so freely and by nature," the feelings of all of the animals would declare that this had been well spoken. It is a disgrace, by Zeus, that the birthings and the labor pains and the upbringings of animals should be a matter of nature and freely given, while among humans they are loans and wages and bribes given in hopes of advantage.

(*On the Love of Offspring* 495A–B)

Animals Are Naturally Just because They Care for Their Offspring Tenderly

SOCLARUS: Well, Autobulus, count me among those who believe what you say. Yet when I compare the behaviors of animals with the characters, lifestyles, activities and modes of conduct of human beings, I observe [in animals] a great want of excellence in other respects and in particular a lack of striving for virtue, on account of which reason was created, and too an absence of progress toward and longing for it. I am at a loss to understand how nature could have given the beginning [of reason] to creatures that are incapable of achieving its completion.

AUTOBULUS: This too does not seem absurd to that group of thinkers. While considering the love of one's offspring to be the origin of fellowship and justice among us, and observing that there is abundant and strong [love of offspring] among animals, they deny and refuse to acknowledge that they share in justice.

(*On the Cleverness of Animals* 962A–B)

Suggestions for Further Reading

Homer

Dierauer, *Tier und Mensch* 7–15.

Körner, Otto, *Die Homerische Tierwelt* (Munich: Bergmann, 1930).

Lilja, Saara, "Theriophily in Homer," *Arctos* 8 (1974) 71–78. Lilja cites numerous examples of Homer's sympathy for the sufferings of animals.

Nicolay, Eveline, "Homère et l'Âme des Bêtes," in Niewöhner and Sebon, eds, *Die Seele Der Tiere* 51–58. This article offers an analysis of Homer's understanding of the souls of animals.

Rahn, Helmut, "Das Tier in der homerischen Dichtung," *Studium Generale* 20 (1967) 90–105. Rahn cautions against studying Homer as a naturalist and therefore expecting exactitude and deep knowledge of animals from his pronouncements on other species.

——, "Tier und Mensch in der homerischen Auffassung der Wirklichkeit," *Paideuma* 5 (1953) 277–297 and 431–480. Rahn here emphasizes how Homer's text reveals its author's conception of the place of both man and animal in the universe.

Cicero

Renehan, Robert, "The Greek Anthropocentric View of Man."

Plutarch

Becchi, "Istinto e Intelligenza negli Scritti Zoopsicologici di Plutarco" 60–70. Here Becchi argues that the contradictions in Plutarch's position on rationality in animals between *On the Love of Offspring* and *On the Cleverness of Animals* have been exaggerated by critics since in both works the degree of rationality in animals vis-à-vis that in human beings, rather than the presence or absence of reason in animals, is the matter at issue.

3. Relation to the Environment: Prey and Predators

The capacity of animals to distinguish between their prey and their natural predators, a matter of live and death immediately upon birth, was perceived by ancient thinkers as a manifestation of the nexus of philosophical ideas embodied in the concept of *oikeiōsis* so fundamental to the Stoic ethical system (see pp. 27–28). While the Stoics judged this recognition of the need for self-preservation and at the same time for community membership to be a matter of natural impulse (*hormē*) in animals (see the formulation of the Stoic position as given in Diogenes Laertius, *Lives of the Philosophers* VII. 85, on p. 28), Plutarch argued that some degree of rationality had to be operative in animals to guarantee that they could recognize the difference between the harmful and the beneficial in their lives (see p. 47).

Philo of Alexandria

Philo's formulation below of the principle that animals shun the harmful combines the Stoic assertion that a desire for self-preservation is a primary motivating factor in animal behavior with the Stoic doctrine that the pursuit of pleasure is natural to animals as well (Diogenes Laertius VII. 85–86), although Philo appears to make the pursuit of pleasure in animals a more important impulse in animals than the Stoics allowed since they argued rather that the desire for self-preservation far outweighed the pursuit of pleasure in animals.

Animals Flee the Harmful

However it is worth noting – for it is obvious – that they have various ways of coping with opposites as well as of facing obstacles. With regard to heat and cold, sweet and bitter, white and black, large and small, or whatever inconveniences result from these opposites, they set their reasoning mind differently toward them, so as to make them pleasant and agreeable. They long for that which produces pleasure and flee from that which is loathsome and painful. Although they are unable to express their mental conceptions because of their inarticulate tongues, they conduct themselves with such abundant wisdom that they exhibit many characteristics of speech. To the keenly perceptive there is something more evident than voice – the truth which their actions reveal.

(On Animals 44)

Seneca

Letter 121 of Seneca's *Moral Letters* contains his longest continuous discussion of the nature of animal intellect. In common with his Stoic brethren, Seneca denied reason to non-human animals, but in the selection below, he concedes to them at least as "consciousness of their own constitution" (*constitutionis suae sensus*, 121. 5), the presence of which in animals is proven by their ability to move their limbs appropriately and readily, as if trained to do so. The philosopher's imaginary interlocutor in the letter observes that Seneca seems to equate this constitution, which the animal understands by nature, with the "principle of the soul." The interlocutor refers here to the so-called *hēgemonikon* identified in Stoic philosophy (see pp. 3–4), which, he maintains, is a concept so subtle in nature that a human being can scarcely grasp its meaning. Seneca replies that the animal understands its own constitution rather than the concept of a constitution. The doctrine that underlies Seneca's arguments here is that of *oikeiōsis*, which enables an animal from birth to recognize what is appropriate to itself. No sophisticated mental faculties, therefore, need to be attributed to an animal's understanding of its own constitution.

Animal Self-Preservation Is Based on Self-Awareness

Someone asserts, "Animals move the parts of their bodies appropriately because if they should move otherwise, they would feel pain. Hence as you [philosophers] say, they are under compulsion, and fear, not will, moves them correctly." This is false. Those things that are propelled by a force are slow, while those that move on their own possess quickness. So utterly untrue it is that fear of pain moves them that they even struggle to perform their natural motion when pain inhibits them. Thus an infant who is intent on standing up and is becoming used to his own weight falls and gets up repeatedly, in tears, until, in the midst of the pain, he has trained himself to that which nature requires. Certain animals that have hard shells, when turned over, twist themselves and thrust out their legs and bend about until they are restored to a proper position. A tortoise when on its back feels no pain, but is restless on account of its desire for its normal position, and it does not cease to struggle and shake itself about until it has reestablished its footing. Thus all creatures have an understanding of their own constitution (*constitutionis*) and thus can use their limbs so easily, and we have no greater proof that they come into life armed with knowledge than the fact that no animal is clumsy in the use of its own self.

Someone objects, "The constitution, as you would argue, is the governing principle of the soul which has a particular relationship with the body. How does an infant understand this very complex and subtle notion that can scarcely be explained to you? All animals would have to be born capable of understanding logic to be able to comprehend this definition which is difficult for the vast majority of citizens." What you object would be true if I claimed that the *definition of the constitution* was understood by animals, rather than the *constitution itself*. Nature is more readily understood than explained. Thus an infant does not understand what a "constitution" is, but he understands *his own* constitution. He does not know what an animal is, but senses that he is an animal. We know that we have a soul, but we do not know what it is, or where it resides, or what its nature is, or whence it arises. Just as consciousness of our soul passes to us, though we do not know its nature or location, so is there a consciousness of their constitution in all animals. It is necessary that they should be conscious of that through which they are conscious of other things as well, and that they have a consciousness of that which they obey and by which they are governed. There is no human who does not know that there is something that excites his impulses, but he is ignorant as to what that is. Thus both infants and animals possess a consciousness of their primary element which is not too clearly distinct or exact.

(*Moral Letters* 121. 7–13)

Plutarch

In the passage from *On the Cleverness of Animals* translated below, Plutarch offers a somewhat different take on the innate capacity of animals to distinguish those things that are akin to them from those that are foreign to them, arguing that this capacity is not, as the Stoics maintained, a mere function of the operation of instinct (*hormē*), but rather evidence of a degree of rationality. He alludes to Aristotelian teleology when his mouthpiece Autobulus commends the philosopher's position that nothing happens in nature without some end, so that there would be no purpose in creating sentient creatures if they were not designed to exercise that sentience toward some useful end, in this case, toward self-preservation ensured by recognition of the kindred (*oikeiōn*) and the foreign (*allotriōn*).

Plutarch further elaborates his conception of the components of animal sentience by listing such capacities as recollection, memory and expectation. Slightly earlier (*On the Cleverness of Animals* 961B), Plutarch had argued that their rational faculty allows animals to elaborate on their basic ability to distinguish the harmful from the useful through their capacity for memory, which enables them to recall over time what constitutes their prey and their predators and in what sorts of lairs and dens they are likely to be encountered. This long-term recollection of one's proper prey proves, Autobulus argues (961D), that animals after all possess what the Stoics termed "conceptions" (*ennoiai*) which animals put into action when they hunt and need to present before their minds the picture of their proper prey.

The passage below is incorporated, almost without alterations, into the third book of Porphyry's defense of vegetarianism, in the course of the author's argument for rationality in animals in consequence of which, he maintains, human beings owe a debt of justice to animals.

Rationality Helps Animals to Distinguish the Useful from the Harmful

AUTOBULUS: Nature, which [Aristotle and Theophrastus] correctly say does everything for some reason and toward some end, did not create any sentient creature just so that it could sense that it was experiencing something. But since there exist many things that are akin (*oikeiōn*) to it and many that are foreign to it, a creature could not survive for a moment if it had not learned against which things it should guard and with which it should associate. Sensation provides each creature the recognition of both. Among those creatures that were not born to reason (*logizesthai*) and judge and remember and attend, there could exist no instance of pursuing and seizing of things recognized to be useful, or any escape or flight from those things that were dangerous and painful. Among those creatures that you would deprive of expectation, recollection, intention, preparation, hope, fear, inclination and sadness, there would be no need for eyes or ears though they do possess them. It would be preferable to remove all sensation and imagination devoid of usefulness, than to suffer and feel pain and be distressed, if there exists no means with which these experiences may be cast off.

(On the Cleverness of Animals 960E–F = Porphyry, On Abstinence from Animal Flesh III. 21. 5–7)

Suggestions for Further Reading

Philo of Alexandria

Terian, *Philonis Alexandrini de Animalibus* 154–156. In his commentary on *On Animals* 44, Terian offers a useful survey of Greek pronouncements on the importance of pleasure and pain in the lives of animals, including humans.

Seneca

Dierauer, *Tier und Mensch* 207–211. Dierauer analyzes Seneca's argument that an animal's innate ability to use its limbs is a reflection of its self-awareness.

Reydams-Schils, Gretchen, "Human Bonding and *Oikeiōsis* in Roman Stoicism," *OSAPh* 22 (2002) 221–251. The author examines the appearance of the doctrine of *oikeiōsis* in Roman thinkers including Cicero and Seneca.

Plutarch

Caballero, Raúl, "OIKEIΩΣIΣ in Plutarco," in A. Pérez Jiménez, J. García Lopez and R. Ma. Aguilar, eds, *Plutarco, Platón y Aristoteles. Actas del V Congreso Internacional de la I. P. S.* (Madrid: Ediciones Clásicas, 1999) 549–566. Caballero calls attention to Plutarch's debt to Aristotle's conception of animal recollection and perception, and notes that Plutarch almost completely rejects an instinctual element in animal behavior.

4. Helping Behaviors

The apparent capacity and indeed inclination of some animal species to come to the aid of their conspecifics, of other animal species, and even of human beings, was frequently remarked upon by ancient naturalists and catalogers of animal wonders, at least some of whom attempted to interpret the meaning of such actions. Ancient writers described several varieties of helping behaviors, although they did not endeavor to differentiate these by name. One such behavior may be termed "cooperation," an action in which conspecifics work together toward some common goal. Plutarch (*On the Cleverness of Animals* 972B), reports, for example, that the African king and historian Juba related that if an elephant falls into a trap set up by hunters, other elephants will cast stones and wood into the trap to enable their unfortunate colleague to climb out on these objects.

Cooperative behavior of this sort, if performed by human beings, would very likely be termed "altruism" – the sort of helping behavior from which the helpers derive no apparent immediate benefit. Cognitive ethologists, biologists who specialize in the study of animal cognition as it manifests itself in behavior, distinguish altruistic actions from strictly cooperative actions, as, for example, situations in which wolves hunt in packs and all benefit immediately from the kill. Some ethologists isolate a subset of altruism that they call "reciprocal altruism," characterized by a sort of "payback system," in which an animal will perform a service for an animal that had previously helped it. Vampire bats, for example, are known to regurgitate blood to feed bats that had been unsuccessful in securing blood for themselves. Ethologists note that bats that have previously regurgitated blood are more likely to be supplied with blood in this manner than those that have not.

More controversial in recent ethological debate is the question of whether animals are capable of performing helping actions of a sort that might be termed "philanthropic" – that is, whether animals can carry out actions intended to benefit human beings that are carried out from some sense of benevolence toward humans on the part of the animal actors. Only Plutarch, of the authors excerpted below, attributes this intentionality to animals, which some scientists deny can be properly applied at all to animal behaviors. It would, they maintain, necessitate not only a sophisticated level of intellectual activity to understand that another animal, perhaps even one of another species, is in need of aid that the animal forming this thought can provide, and a degree of empathy to appreciate the significance of the distress of other creatures. The issue of particular difficulty to philosophers and ethologists who question the ascription of sophisticated mental states to animals, even to those that seem as intelligent to both ancient and modern investigators as dolphins were acknowledged to be, is that of whether animals are capable of "intentionality" – that is, do animals *intend* to help other creatures, and are they capable of the beliefs, desires, hopes and fears that would inspire such intentions? Ancient naturalists may have witnessed, as have modern ethologists, the sorts of rescues, whether of ailing dolphins or of floundering human swimmers, that are executed by dolphins that swim underneath the endangered creatures and bear them to safety, and, as in the case of modern ethologists who interpret such behaviors, some ancients seem to have been more willing than others to identify the action involved as intentional and guided by the operation of some mental action on the part of the rescuers.

The three passages given below provide a study in contrasts. Each provides a version of a famous anecdote – the rescue at sea of the poet Arion who was forced to cast himself into the sea by greedy sailors eager to steal his earnings from a concert tour. Despite his fondness for the exotic and his tendency to draw moral lessons from anecdotes, Herodotus hardly mentions the dolphin at all, and seems to tell the tale primarily to account for the bronze statue of a boy on a dolphin that closes his version. In Herodotus, one animal effects the rescue and no observation is made as to its motivation.

Dolphins figure prominently in the ninth book of Pliny's *Natural History*, one of the zoological books of his encyclopedia that are replete with wondrous accounts of animal behaviors related by Pliny with obvious gusto, despite his protestations of hesitation to relate them. His version of the tale of Arion takes a middle position between the straightforward narrative of Herodotus and the relatively elaborate interpretation which Plutarch places on the behavior of the animals. Taking it as his thesis that the dolphin is "an animal friendly to man" (*homini … amicum animal, Natural History* IX. 24), Pliny proceeds to demonstrate the truth of this assertion with a selection of anecdotes in which dolphins are treated almost as pets by human beings and, in one instance, are credited with the emotion of grief at the death of a human companion. While cognitive ethology has become increasingly willing to countenance the possibility that some animal species are capable of grief at the death of a conspecific, interspecies emotional attachments have not won wide acceptance in biological circles.

It is instructive to note that, in Pliny's version of the Arion tale, it is their affection for music that initially draws the animals to Arion's ship and that, although a school of dolphins initially approaches the ship, Arion was rescued by a single animal whose motivation is not stated. In the final anecdote from Pliny translated below (IX. 33), the "public-spiritedness" (*publica … societas*) of the animals is commented on, a sort of behavior that ethology would define as cooperation combined with altruism since the animals that together petitioned for the release of their captured comrade not only derived no immediate benefit from their actions but jeopardized their own safety in the process.

In the retelling of the anecdote of Arion's rescue contained in Plutarch's dialogue *Banquet of the Seven Sages*, the most sweeping claims are made for developed intellectual capacity on the part of the animals and for intentionality in their actions. Plutarch's version purports to be an eye-witness account of the rescue given by Gorgus, brother of the tyrant Periander of Corinth, who relates that he and his comrades observed a school of dolphins gathering about the drowning singer and carrying him to safety on shore, acting, he maintains, as if they considered this action "a duty necessary and incumbent upon them all in turn" (hōs anagkaion en merei leitourgēma kai prosēkon pāsin, Banquet of the Seven Sages 161D). Only in Plutarch's version is the rescue effected by more than one animal, an addition which allows Plutarch to introduce the idea of cooperative action, and it is particularly striking that Plutarch employs language heavily charged with ethical overtones in his suggestion that the animals believed their action "incumbent" upon them all. Plutarch judges the dolphin to be a creature capable of disinterested helpful action directed toward another animal species that is carried out with purpose and clear intentionality. It is worth noting that, shortly after his retelling of the anecdote of Arion, Plutarch relates how dolphins bore to shore the body of the poet Hesiod, an action which, he declares, the animals performed in a "kindred and human-loving manner" (oikeiōs kai philanthrōpōs, Banquet of the Seven Sages 162F). In Plutarch's estimation, some animal species are capable even of actions that, if performed by human beings, one would readily term "philanthropic," and it is remarkable that Plutarch here juxtaposes this idea with the concept of oikeiōsis, the sense of relationship and kinship which the Stoics denied between humans and animals but which Plutarch allowed to exist on an interspecies level (see pp. 32–33), suggesting that he believed that human–animal kinship can lead animals with developed intellectual capacities, such as dolphins, to intervene on behalf of human beings.

Herodotus

Arion Rescued by a Dolphin

Periander was tyrant of Corinth. The Corinthians, with whom the Lesbians agree, tell of a great marvel in his lifetime, namely that Arion of Methymna was carried on a dolphin to Taenarum. As a dithyrambist, he was second to none, and we know that he first invented the form and named it and taught it in Corinth. They say that this Arion, who had spent a great deal of time at the court of Periander, desired to sail to Italy and Sicily and, after making a lot of money there, to return to Corinth. He sailed from Taenarum after hiring a ship of Corinthian sailors because he trusted no one more than Corinthians, but when they were at sea, the Corinthians plotted against Arion to steal his money after casting him overboard. They say that when he realized this, he beseeched them to take his money but to allow him to live. He could not win them over, but the boatmen ordered him either to kill himself so he could have a grave on land, or to jump into the sea as quickly as possible. Forced to dire straits, he asked them, since this was their intention, to allow him to stand on the rowing benches and to sing, in full dress. He promised to do away with himself after singing. The boatmen were delighted at the prospect of hearing the best singer among men perform, and they withdrew into the middle of the ship. Putting on his robes and taking up his lyre, he stood in the benches and performed the high-pitched mode of singing. When the song was finished, he threw himself into the sea, just as he was, in full costume.

They say the sailors returned to Corinth, but that a dolphin picked Arion up and carried him to Taenarum. Landing there, he went, in costume, to Corinth and reported the entire incident. Because he did not believe him, Periander arrested him and would not set him free, and kept an eye out for the seamen. When they arrived, he sent for them and asked if they had anything to say about Arion. When they said that he was safe in Italy and that they had left him faring well in Tarentum, he appeared before them, looking as he had on jumping overboard. Astounded, the seamen had nothing to say in denial when thus refuted. The Corinthians and Lesbians tell this tale, and there exists now in Taenarum a bronze statue, of no great size, of a man on a dolphin.

(Histories I. 23–24)

Pliny the Elder

Philanthropic Deeds of Dolphins

The dolphin is an animal that is not only fond of humans but is enchanted as well by music, especially by the harmony of instruments and above all by the water organ. It does not fear the human being as something alien to itself, but comes to meet vessels and plays joyfully about them, entering into competition with them and passing them even when they are under full sail. In the reign of the deified Augustus, a dolphin introduced into the Lucrine Lake loved, with a peculiar attachment, a certain poor man's son who went from the Baiae region to school in Pozzuoli. The boy who hung about the area at noontime called the animal Snubnose and rather often lured the dolphin with bread that he carried for his journey (I would be ashamed to tell the tale if it were not related by Maecenas, Fabianus, Flavius Alfius, and many others). At whatever time of day the animal was summoned by the boy, it would fly to him from the depths, even if it had been hidden and out of sight, and, after eating out of his hand, would offer him its back to climb aboard, carrying him to class in Pozzuoli, while hiding his spines in a sort of sheath, and carrying him back in a similar manner for several years. When the boy eventually died of illness, the animal, coming back to its accustomed place in sadness, in the manner of a mourner, died itself, out of grief, which no one doubted.

(Natural History IX. 24–25)

The people of Amphilochus and Tarentum tell similar tales about boys and dolphins. They make it possible for us to believe that Arion, famous for his cithara, when sailors on the high sea were preparing to kill him and seize his money, coaxed them to allow him to play the cithara first. A school of dolphins was drawn by his playing, and when he jumped into the sea, he was taken up by one and carried to the shore at Tarentum.

(Natural History IX. 28)

Dolphins possess public spiritedness among themselves. When one was captured by the King of Caria and tied up in the harbor, a great multitude of its fellows came together and begged for mercy, with a palpable sense of sorrow, until the king ordered the animal to be let go. In truth, some larger animal always accompanies a smaller one, in the manner of an attendant, and some have been seen carrying a dead comrade so that it could not be torn apart by sea beasts.

(Natural History IX. 33)

Plutarch

Animals That Help Humans and Each Other

Gorgus told us that his sacrifice took three days and on the last of these, there was a nightlong dance and choral performance and games by the shore. The moon shone upon the sea, and there was no wind but rather a stillness and calm. From far off, a rippling effect was noticed advancing toward the headland bringing some foam and a lot of noise with its rustling movement so that everyone ran down in amazement to the place where it was approaching. Before they could guess what was approaching so quickly, dolphins were seen, some circling about in crowds, others leading a path to the smoothest area of the shore, and still others in the rear like a guard. Among them, above the top of the water's surface, was an indistinct and obscure mass of a body being borne along. Eventually the dolphins came together, and landing as a group, put on shore a man who was breathing and moving. Thereupon the dolphins, bearing out toward the headland again, leapt up more than before, playing out of joy, it appeared, and jumping about.

"Many of us," Gordus said, "fled away from the sea in confusion, but a few, including myself, were brave enough to approach, and recognized Arion the cithara player who told us his name himself, though he was clearly recognizable from his outfit (he happened to be wearing the outfit he wore when he performed). We accompanied him to the tent, there appearing to be nothing wrong with him except that he seemed to be exhausted and disconcerted by the speed and noise of his ride, and we heard from him a story incredible except to us who had seen its conclusion. Arion said that he had determined to set out from Italy, and after Periander wrote to him, he became more enthusiastic about the venture. When a Corinthian vessel appeared, he embarked and shipped out. After they had sailed three days under a moderate breeze, Arion sensed that the sailors were plotting to throw him over, and he learned secretly from the helmsman that it had been determined to do this that night.

Abandoned and not knowing what to do, he had a sort of divine inspiration to adorn his person and to take as his funeral garment, while still living, the outfit that he used in performance, singing his life away and thereby proving no less noble than the swan. After dressing and announcing that he had conceived a certain desire to sing in the Pythian mode for the sake of his safety and that of the ship and its crew, he stood along the side in the stern, and after performing a sort of invocation to the gods of the sea, he sang his ode. He was not half finished when the sun dipped into the sea and the Peloponnesus became visible. The sailors did not wait any longer for the coming of night, but proceeded to the murder.

Seeing drawn knives and the covered head of the helmsman, Arion ran back and threw himself as far as possible from the ship. Before his body was completely submerged, dolphins swam up under him and carried him upward, filled as he was at first with distress and tumult. But when he became comfortable in being carried, and when he saw many animals gathered about him in a kindly manner, and taking him up as if it were a duty necessary and incumbent upon all of them in turn, and when the distance of the ship afforded him some sense of their speed, he said that he felt not so much fear of death or desire to live as an eagerness to be saved so that he might be seen to be a man loved by the gods and might receive from the gods a secure reputation.

(Septem Sapientium Convivium [Banquet of the Seven Sages] 160E–161E)

Suggestions for Further Reading

Hauser, Marc D., *Wild Minds: What Animals Really Think* (New York: Henry Holt, 2000) 210–253. Hauser here discusses the possibility of moral instincts in non-human animals, including the issue of whether non-humans can be moral agents, the sorts of creatures that act according to a set of moral values and with a sense of respect for the values of other agents.

Newmyer, *Animals, Rights and Reason in Plutarch and Modern Ethics* 76–84. Chapter Five, "Beauty in the Beast: Cooperation, Altruism and Philanthropy among Animals," discusses the meanings of helping behaviors in non-human species and attempts to differentiate among the sorts of helping behaviors that ancient naturalists and modern ethologists have observed.

———, "Animal *Philanthropia* in the *Convivium Septem Sapientium*," in José Ribeiro, Delfim Leão, Manuel Tröster and Paula Barata Dias, eds, *Symposion and Philanthropia in Plutarch* (Coimbra: Centro de Estudos Clássicas e Humanísticos da Universidade de Coimbra, 2009) 497–504. This study analyzes in detail Plutarch's assertions of the ethical dimensions of dolphin behaviors.

Steiner, Gary, *Animals and the Moral Community: Mental Life, Moral Status, and Kinship* (New York: Columbia University Press, 2008). Steiner offers a thorough-going critique of the idea of intentionality in non-human animals.

van der Stockt, Luc, "Plutarch and Dolphins: Love Is All You Need," in Boulogne, ed., *Les Grecs et les Animaux: Le Cas Remarquable de Plutarque* 13–21. Van der Stockt argues that the dolphins that rescue Arion in Plutarch's version act as agents of God performing actions that illustrate God's love for all of his creatures, and not from a sense of kinship or love of humans.

deWaal, Frans, *Good Natured: The Origins of Right and Wrong in Humans and Other Animals* (Cambridge, MA: Harvard University Press, 1996). The ethologist deWaal argues for an elemental sense of morality in some non-human animals.

———, *The Age of Empathy: Nature's Lessons for a Kinder Society* (New York: Harmony Books, 2009). DeWaal argues here that examination of the social behaviors of animals indicates that both human and non-human species are preprogrammed by nature to reach out to aid other animals. Modern instances of dolphin rescues of human beings are discussed.

5. Skills and Shortcomings

Xenophon

Although it is impossible to know to what extent the ideas expressed in the passage below from Xenophon's *Memorabilia* (*Recollections of Socrates*), a four-volume collection of Xenophon's memories of what he heard his mentor Socrates say on a variety of topics, is a faithful reflection of the Master's views, the passage is in any case remarkable for its thorough-going anthropocentrism and its articulation, relatively early in the history of Greek speculation on the nature of animalkind, of a number of what would in time become standard arguments in the arsenal of those who, like the Stoics, sought to prove that man is physically and mentally superior to other animals and is held in special regard by his creator. The passage is particularly striking for showing no traces of the usual classical concession of superiority to animals in such capacities as physical stamina, strength, keenness of the senses and natural protection of the body by hair and claws (for a particularly interesting formulation of this idea, see Plato, *Protagoras* 320c–322d). Here in Xenophon, humans are declared superior to other species in every aspect of life.

Xenophon's exposition offers manifestations of a number of the standard claims in what we designated above (see p. 12) as the "man alone of animals" commonplace, so frequently encountered in classical discussions of the nature of animalkind: that only man has upright posture (repeated in Plato, *Timaeus* 91e–92a, and in Philo, *On Animals* 11); that only man has articulate language (see pp. 60–62); and that only man engages in sexual activity year round (repeated in Philo, *On Animals* 49; Plutarch, *Gryllus* 990D; and Pliny, *Natural History* X. 83. 171).

Xenophon's final claim of particular excellence in the human being introduces the thesis of the second part of his exposition, an idea that would later resonate with the Stoic school in the formulation of its own account of human–animal relations: man is given a superior soul, which proves the special favor in which humans are held by the gods in the order of creation. This allows humans, alone of animals, to contemplate the divine, a claim that would itself come to be challenged (see, for example, Plutarch, *On the Cleverness of Animals* 972B; Pliny, *Natural History* VIII. 1. 2–3; and Aelian, *On the Nature of Animals* VII. 4).

Shortcomings of Animal Anatomy and Intellect

SOCRATES: "Do you not then suppose that [the gods] take heed of man? In the first place, they have endowed man, alone among animals, with upright posture. Upright posture enables man to see more things above and ahead, and allows our vision and hearing and face to be exposed to less danger. Secondly, to other animals that move about they have given feet that allow them merely to move, while to man they give in addition hands which effect most of those actions that cause us to be happier than these other creatures. And they gave man a tongue (an organ which all animals possess) which, by touching one or another part of the mouth, is uniquely able to articulate the voice and signal all we wish to one another. For other animals they have defined a distinct time of year to devote to sexual pleasures, while to us they allow this activity continually into old age.

Nor was god satisfied to care only for the human body, but (and this is the greatest thing of all) he implanted in man the most excellent soul. What other animal's soul has perceived that the gods, who have put in order the greatest and finest of things, do exist? What race of creatures other than man worships the gods? What soul is more capable than man's of guarding against hunger or thirst or cold or heat, or of fighting off illness, or of promoting good health, or of working toward knowledge, or of remembering what one might hear or see or learn? Is it not plain to you that, in comparison to other animals, men live like gods, most excellent by nature in body and soul? For with the body of an ox and the mind of a man, one could not do what one wished, since that which has hands but no reason has nothing more. Do you not then suppose that, having received the two gifts which are more valuable, you are in god's care?"

(*Memorabilia* [*Recollections of Socrates*] I. 4. 11–14)

Philo of Alexandria

The everyday activities of even the smallest animals proved endlessly fascinating to ancient philosophers and naturalists. Some who sought to demonstrate the presence of at least a modicum of rational activity in animal species cited, with stereotypic regularity, the construction of elaborate webs by spiders, the highly developed cooperation of ant and bee societies, and the painstaking nest building and prudent rearing of nestlings by swallows as evidence of purposeful activities guided by the operation of some intelligence (see pp. 17–19). Others, especially those writing under the influence of Stoic conceptions of animal motivation, attributed these activities to "nature" (*phusis*), what later biologists would label "instinct."

Proponents of the belief that animals are rational, moreover, judged such apparent examples of technical skill, diligence, foresight and determination, to be evidence of "virtues" (*aretai*) operational in certain animal species, while they often took other animal actions, including aggression, timidity and ferocity, to be "vices" (*kakiai*) in animals. Indeed, the very presence of such "vices" argued, in their view, for the presence of reason in animals, since, they concluded, only creatures capable of acting in accord with reason (that is, virtuously) could demonstrate the opposite of rational behavior (that is, vice). Philo's nephew Alexander opens his discussion of vices in animals with a statement of this position (*On Animals* 66).

Immediately preceding this section, Alexander had argued at length (*On Animals* 30–65) that animals demonstrate, in varying degrees and according to species, the cardinal virtues set forth by Plato in *Republic* 427–445e: wisdom (*sophia*); courage (*andreia*); restraint (*sōphrosynē*); and justice (*dikaiosynē*). Alexander next turns to an exposition of animal vices (*On Animals* 66–70). The vices that Alexander identifies in these paragraphs (thoughtlessness, cowardice, lack of restraint and injustice) are behaviors directly opposed to the original Platonic virtues. Alexander concludes his treatment of animal vices, and his exposition altogether, in Section 71, wherein he reiterates his position that animals have both virtues and vices in consequence of their having, like human beings, the faculty of reason.

Alexander's remarks in the selections below appear to be directed against the Stoic conception of virtue and vice, according to which animals cannot exercise desire (*orexis*), a rational impulse that aims at the good. Animal actions are inspired rather by impulse (*hormē*), and are concerned strictly with matters of self-preservation. Consequently, it is not possible to speak of virtues in the case of animals any more than one can speak of vices in them.

In Section 77, Philo is imagined as taking up his rebuttal, brief and rather spiritless as it is (*On Animals* 77–100), of the arguments set forth in the exposition of Alexander's lecture in defense of rationality in animals. Philo's refutation opens with one of the treatise's few overt appeals to religion, and proceeds to a rehearsal of standard examples of apparent rational activity in animals that parallel those mentioned in Alexander's lecture. Philo argues that such activities do not argue for the presence of any degree of rational activity in animals but suggest rather the operation of "nature" (*phusis*), a position closely aligned with Stoic doctrine. It is striking that Philo ends his comments here (Section 78) with a suggestion that animals are no more skilled than are plants. His position ends up being even more severe than that of most Stoics who conceded such capacities as impulse (*hormē*) and perceptual appearance (*phantasia*) to animals but not to plants.

Vices of Animals

Moreover vices, no less than virtues, are indications of innate reason. I have little need to show similarities of faults between man and other animals: folly, lack of self-restraint, cowardice, injustice, all that are related to these, and numerous common debaucheries. However animals have been left destitute of truth. Some of them are sly, for example, wolves and foxes. Likewise he-goats and pigeons are lewd in sexual relations. Indeed they possess a frantic ardor. The male pigeon has a habit of breaking the eggs and keeps hovering about while the female sits on the eggs. When they are seized with wild passion, they do not confine themselves to their own species. Instead they rush deviously into perversions because of insatiability. ...

Some animals are so fearful that they succumb to the weakest ones and are terrified by the shadow of the mighty. There are those that hide fearfully in cavernous mountains and valleys and in thick forests and others in the thickets of woods in high places, turning their faces as they watch here and there. Only of the flight of birds are they not afraid. Deer confirm my words. Apparently when their cowardice was first found out by nature, they were given large defensive weapons. Unlike other animals which have two horns attached to their heads, deer have many branches on theirs, growing here and there like boughs from a tree trunk. Since they are in desperate need to defend themselves, their armament has to be appropriately large. But what does it profit cowards to be powerfully armed? Not even ornaments make ugly women look beautiful. Therefore it is very shameful to make oneself gaudy with ornaments. ...

Just as these animals are stricken with dread, others have allowed themselves to grow shamelessly and insolently daring. Is it necessary to talk about the aggressiveness of wild boars, leopards, and lions in being ready to act unjustly and to injure? Even the dog, though this animal is fed by man, charges at strange faces and is frantic and fierce. If it happens to see someone very far away, it howls incessantly, and of course, barks as it attacks. When it gets close enough, it charges, unmindful of all the injuries which it might suffer. It assaults very furiously, staring with bloody eyes, its mouth full of froth. Not only does it withstand rocks thrown at it, but it also defies the strikes of lances and arrows and keeps advancing in spite of them.

(On Animals 66, 68, 70)

Instinct in Animals

PHILO: For my part Lysimachus, I am ready. But take care that by such questioning and surmising we do not sin against the sacred mind. What about the spiders which are considered to be weavers and others, the bees, which make honeycombs? They do this neither by means of skill nor by innate reason. They have no particular accomplishment, to tell the truth, except that they work diligently. For since art is an acquired skill, what accomplishment is there when there has been no previously acquired knowledge which is the basis of the arts?

Now for example, birds fly, aquatics swim, and terrestrials walk. Is this done by learning? Certainly not. Each of the above mentioned creatures does it by its nature.

Likewise bees make honeycombs by nature, not by learning. Spiders also make their fine work of lace spontaneously. If one wishes to be dissuaded from wrong thinking about creatures, he should go to look at the trees and notice every intricate detail. These too have many aesthetic features but no skill in the arts.

(On Animals 77–78)

Plutarch

In the first passage below from Plutarch's dialogue *On the Cleverness of Animals*, his Stoic mouthpiece Soclarus admits to Aristotimus, who defends the position that animals possess some degree of reason, that he has convinced him that animals do indeed exhibit perception and some emotions, but he denies them any inclination toward virtue (*aretē*) or any ability to attain it. This strikes Soclarus as contradictory since the purpose of reason is to enable the creature possessing it to strive toward virtue, and it is therefore absurd for nature to have accorded animals the beginnings of reason if they are incapable of attaining the fullness of reason. Soclarus' argument here shows clear evidence of a knowledge of Stoic technical vocabulary: the Stoics denied that animals could manifest a "striving" or "desire" (*orexis*) for virtue since *orexis* was regarded by them as a function of reason and they reckoned animals irrational. "Progress" (*prokopē*) is made by the rational being on his road to wisdom and away from folly, a journey which Soclarus declares to be impossible for animals.

In his reply, Autobulus notes that while the Stoics acknowledge that animals love their offspring and that such love is the origin of the virtue called justice, they still deny justice to animals. The mistake of the Stoics, he argues (*On the Cleverness of Animals* 962C), is to mistake the imperfection of virtue in animals with its absence. Indeed, not even all human beings can attain to the perfection of reason, which is the product of education and careful tending. Likewise, it is a mistake to declare that animals that are not intended by nature to attain to the fullness of reason have therefore no reason at all. Some animals are more advanced on the path toward virtue than are others, which is equally true of human beings (963A).

In his survey of animal skills (*On the Cleverness of Animals* 974A–B, D–E), Plutarch's Aristotimus reiterates a number of the standard examples for evidence of innate reason in animals (web making, nest building), but he expands on two such arguments which are less frequently encountered in ancient sources though not unparalleled: an innate understanding in animals of the healing art, and an understanding of number. Philo (*On Animals* 38) allows his interlocutor Alexander to claim that an understanding of medicine is more natural to non-human animals because they do not need, unlike human beings, to consult a physician to secure a diagnosis, but know by nature the correct course of action.

Aristotimus' claim that animals have a knowledge of number is denied by Aristotle (*Topica* 142b23–28), but Plutarch's anecdote of cattle in Susa that can count is repeated in Aelian, *Nature of Animals* VII. 1. The computational skill of non-human animals is currently the subject of investigation by cognitive etholo-gists, some of whom have concluded that certain bird species and chimpanzees appear to be able to make elementary judgments about number, although there is still no agreement among investigators as to what such a capacity might signify.

Moral Failings in Animals

SOCLARUS: Well, Autobulus, count me among those you have convinced. Yet on comparing human conduct and lifestyles and practices and behaviors with those of animals, I see many other weaknesses [in animals], and in particular a lack of any clear evidence of concern for virtue, for which reason was created, nor any progress or striv-ing toward it. I wonder how nature can have given the beginnings of reason to creatures incapable of attaining its end.

(*On the Cleverness of Animals* 962A)

A Survey of Animal Skills

ARISTOTIMUS: Perhaps we are foolish to exult over the learning of animals, when Democritus makes clear that we are their pupils in the greatest matters. We are pupils of spiders in the arts of weaving and mending, of the swallow in home construction, and of sweet-voiced swans and nightingales in our imitation of their song. We see in them a goodly portion of each of the three branches of the healing art, for they do not avail themselves solely of the art of drugs. When they have eaten a snake, tortoises then eat marjoram and weasels eat rue. Dogs eat grass to purge themselves when they are nauseous. ... And too they say that elephants practice surgery. Standing by their wounded comrades, they readily and harmlessly, with no tearing of flesh, withdraw spears, lances and arrows. Cretan goats, by eating dittany, easily expel arrows, sup-plying a simple lesson to pregnant women that that herb has abortive powers. When they are wounded, there is no substance but dittany that goats seek and go after in preference.

Though this is wondrous, it is less so than the fact that some creatures have a knowl-edge of number and a power to count, as do the cattle of Susa. They water the royal park with wheeled water buckets, and the number of bucketfuls is prescribed. Each cow carries one hundred buckets each day, and it is not possible to trick them or force them to carry more. Though people have tried, as an experiment, to add to the total on many occasions, they balk and will not move when once they have done their quota. So accurately does a cow count, as Ktesias the Knidian has related.

(*On the Cleverness of Animals* 974A–B, D–E)

Suggestions for Further Reading

Xenophon

Dierauer, *Tier und Mensch* 48–59. Dierauer here provides a survey of Greek notions about the relative physical and psychical strengths and weaknesses of human beings vis-à-vis other animal species.

Newmyer, Stephen T., "Paws to Reflect: Ancients and Moderns on the Religious Sensibilities of Animals." Assertions of religious leanings in non-human animals found in

Pliny, Plutarch and Aelian are explored, with discussion of the claim in modern ethological literature.

Renehan, "The Greek Anthropocentric View of Man." Renehan supplies extensive citations from classical literature that argue that human beings are unique in possessing some physical or intellectual advantage over other species.

Philo of Alexandria

Dickerman, "Some Stock Illustrations of Animal Intelligence."

Newmyer, *Animals, Rights and Reason in Plutarch and Modern Ethics* 36–39. Stoic concepts of virtue and vice are discussed as these pertain to the lives of animals.

Steiner, *Anthropocentrism and Its Discontents* (Pittsburgh: University of Pittsburgh Press, 2005) 81–88. Steiner offers an overview of Stoic notions on animal skills and their meaning in Stoic ethics.

Terian, *Philonis Alexandrini de Animalibus.* Terian's commentary on Sections 66–70 of *On Animals* provides references to discussions of animal vices in other ancient sources, along with parallels to passages elsewhere in Philo.

Plutarch

Martos Montiel, Juan Francisco, "*Sophrosyne* o *Akrasía*: Los Animales como Modelo de Comportamiento en los *Moralia* de Plutarco," in José Antonio Fernández Delgado and Francisca Pordomingo Pardo, eds, *Estudios sobre Plutarco: Aspectos Formales* (Salamanca: Ediciones Clásicas, 1996) 205–210. This study analyzes Plutarch's use of non-human animals both as ethical models for human behavior and as examples of conduct to be avoided in human life.

Newmyer, Stephen T., "Calculating Creatures: Ancients and Moderns on Understanding of Number in Animals," *QUCC* 89, 2 (2008) 117–124. Classical claims of knowledge of number in animals are examined in light of modern ethological speculation on this phenomenon.

6. The Language of Animals

Diogenes Laertius

Of all the physical and intellectual capacities declared by ancient writers to be unique to human beings, none was so frequently singled out or so vehemently asserted as the human capacity for meaningful language. Indeed, the assertion that man alone of animals is capable of articulate speech still figures prominently in the arsenal of arguments marshaled by cognitive ethologists and philosophers who seek to deny rationality to non-human species and who use what they perceive to be evidence of inferiority in other animal species to deny them a place in the sphere of human moral concern. Some contemporary ethicists argue that communication via symbolic language is a prerequisite for moral status, and that beings can have no claim on such status if they cannot assert their claim to others through meaningful language. As was noted in our discussion of Epicurean attitudes toward animals (see pp. 28–29), the idea that morality is based upon an agreement between individuals to respect each other's interests, is fundamental to modern Contractualism or Contract Theory, in which language is presupposed as the origin of morality and the users of language are presupposed to be rational. Animals, as non-linguistic beings, fall outside the purview of Contractualist ethics.

The intellectual underpinnings of Contractualism can be traced in part to Stoic notions on animal rationality. Noting that the Greek word *logos* means both language and reason, the Stoics argued that since animals lack the one type of *logos*, namely "reason," they consequently lack the other *logos*, "speech." The lack of language in animals arose, in their view, from an imperfection which they identified in the animal soul (*psuchē*). Although they allowed that both human and animal souls were similarly constituted at birth, each having eight parts, they asserted that the eighth part, which they called the *hēgemonikon*, or "governing principle" (on the *hēgemonikon*, see pp. 3–4 and 11–12), develops into the faculty of reason in humans, while that of animals remains forever irrational, thereby denying animals the capacity for meaningful language, since that arose from the rational *hēgemonikon*. In animals, by contrast, vocalizations arise from the operation of impulse (*hormē*), the factor which inspires the actions of non-rational animals. Here the other sense of the Greek term *logos* comes into play since the "internal reason" (*logos endiathetos*) which humans possess in consequence of their being rational and which might be called "thought," gives rise to "external reason" (*logos prophorikos*), a sort of vocalized reason, or meaningful language, arising from the *hēgemonikon*.

In the passage below, Diogenes Laertius alludes to the theory of language production espoused by the influential Stoic Chrysippus who occupied an important place in the development of Stoic ideas on animal intellect (on Chrysippus, see pp. 3–4). Diogenes mentions both the Stoic doctrine of the operation of impulse (*hormē*) on animal actions and the belief that human utterances are the product of reason, which develops, in the view of Chrysippus, when the human attains his fourteenth year.

The Stoics Say That Animal Utterances Are Meaningless

Most of [the Stoics] are in agreement in taking the issue of voice as the starting point for their theory of dialectic. Voice is either percussed air or that thing which is properly perceived by the sense of hearing, as Diogenes the Babylonian says in his treatise *On the Voice*. The voice of an animal is air percussed by impulse, but the voice of a human is, as Diogenes says, articulate and issuing from reason, which matures at age fourteen. According to the Stoics, the voice is a corporeal substance, as Archedemus says in his treatise *On the Voice*, and as Diogenes and Antipater agree, a well as does Chrysippus in the second book of his treatise *On Physics*.

(*Lives of the Philosophers* VII. 55 [from the life of
Zeno the Stoic])

Aristotle

Aristotle denied speech (*logos*) to non-human animals (*Politics* 1253a10–11, translated, p. 75), but he was willing to concede that animals, including all species of birds, have at least the capacity, through their vocalizations, to communicate to their conspecifics an idea of that which is advantageous and pleasant and that which is harmful and painful (*Politics* 1253a11–14). This capacity does not rise, in Aristotle's view, to the level of language because words are not involved in the process. Words must arise from an agreement on the part of those who use them as to their meanings – that is, words are a matter of convention, and such agreement lies outside the scope of non-human intellect (*On Interpretation* 16a28–29). Aristotle does not appear to have believed that other animal species were capable of conveying a notion of anything beyond the pleasant and the painful, but the passage below seems to suggest that he considered the utterances of birds to be capable of imparting some other sorts of information beyond that which is imparted by the utterances of other animal species.

Perhaps Some Animal Utterances Are Meaningful

All [birds] use their tongues for communication with one another, some more so than others, so that it is likely that there is some information conveyed by some of them to the others. I have spoken of these in my books on animals. Most of the land-dwelling ones that lay eggs and are red-blooded have a tongue that is useless for the production of speech because it is both fastened down and hard.

(*Parts of Animals* 660a35–660b2)

Philo of Alexandria

The passage below constitutes Philo's rejoinder to his nephew Alexander's exposition of the two types of reason, *logos endiathetos* and *logos prophorikos*, set forth by Alexander in paragraph 12 of *On Animals* (see p. 13). Whereas Alexander had argued in the earlier passage that both types of reason are present in animals, if in an imperfect state, Philo here counters that the vocalizations of animals, including those of the types of birds generally reckoned most intelligent in ancient sources, the corvids (crows) and parrots, are without meaning. Only humans, he argues, are capable of articulated vocalizations that amount to language, while the sounds that animals produce, because they do not issue from reason, are like musical notes that possess sound but no meaning beyond that.

Animal Utterances Are Meaningless

Now what has been said about mental reasoning suffices: we must next consider the uttered. Although blackbirds, crows, parrots, and all the like can produce different kinds of utterances, they cannot produce an articulated voice in any matter whatever. Furthermore I think that the holes of wind instruments have a marked similarity, for certainly the powerful sounds they release are unintelligible, coarse, and not clearly explained. So also are the meaningless and insignificant sounds produced by the animals previously mentioned. These are not so much real expressions of conceptual words as they are chirps.

(On Animals 98)

Plutarch

In the first passage below, Plutarch offers a spirited and slightly amusing refutation of the Stoic contention that animals are devoid of *logos endiathetos*, "internal reason," and are in consequence incapable of *logos prophorikos*, "meaningful speech." Employing here a frequent strategy of his, Plutarch uses the same examples and technical vocabulary employed by his philosophical rivals, often the Stoics, to arrive at a diametrically opposite conclusion, in many cases by carrying their argument to its logical end. As in Philo's Stoic-inspired exposition, Plutarch cites the vocalizations of corvids, here jays and crows, to provide a concrete example of how *logos endiathetos* in birds gives rise to *logos prophorikos*, meaningful utterance.

As is so often the case in ancient discussions of animal behavior and its interpretation, Plutarch relies on a combination of anecdote and anthropomorphization to explain what led the jay first to fall silent and then to employ vocalizations again. The prolonged silence adopted by the bird was not the result of deafness induced by the blare of funeral trumpets or of poisoning by rival bird trainers but was rather the result of conscious choice on the part of the bird to master the articulations peculiar to the trumpet's music, while it chose at the same time to suppress its customary imitative sounds. In the terms of Stoic linguistic theory, the "internal reason" of the animal, through a process of "self-instruction" (*automatheian*, 973E), which Plutarch declares to be "stronger evidence of reason" (*logikoteran*, 973E) in animals than the mere ability to learn from others, enabled the bird to give voice to the "external reason" of deliberately chosen sounds.

The presupposition of much ancient speculation on animal vocalizations is that, however effective they may be in enabling animals to communicate notions such as pleasure and pain, they nevertheless do not rise to the level of language. Although more developed in the passages from Sextus Empiricus and Porphyry translated below, Plutarch hints, in a manner both fanciful and gruesome, at the idea that animals have meaningful language, in his defense of the vegetarian lifestyle, *On the Eating of Flesh*. Although his main focus in the excerpt below is his notion that a relationship of justice exists between human and non-human animals, he envisions an animal about to be slaughtered for food uttering pleas for justice (*dikaiologias*) in a language that human beings mistakenly take for inarticulate, meaningless vocalizations. Plutarch touches upon an idea developed at greater length by Sextus and Porphyry that the problem in communication lies with human beings, not with animals, since we fail to understand what is in fact a meaningful language that we have simply not yet mastered.

Animal Speech Issues from Reason and Is Perfectible

ARISTOTIMUS: Starlings and crows and parrots which learn to talk and supply their teachers with so easily-molded and imitative an expression of voice to set free and train, seem to me to serve as advocates and supporters to other animals in their learning, instructing us, in some manner, that they have a share of uttered reason and articulate speech. It is therefore supremely ridiculous to compare them with creatures that do not have even enough voice to roar or groan. What charm and music there is in their self-generated and untaught sounds is testified to by the most learned and eloquent writers who compare their sweetest poems to the songs of swans and nightingales. Now since teaching involves more use of reason than does learning, we must trust Aristotle when he says that animals do [teach]. He says that a nightingale had been observed teaching her nestling to sing. A proof of this is the fact that the ability to sing is weaker in the case of those little ones that are reared apart from their mothers, for those that are reared with their mothers are taught and learn, not from a concern for glory or fame, but for the joy involved in tuneful rivalry and because of the love of the beauty rather than of the usefulness of their speech.

I can tell you a story about this that I heard from many Greeks and Romans who were present when it happened. A certain barber at Rome who had a shop in front of the precinct called the Market of the Greeks trained a marvelous jay that was capable of many sounds and notes and would reproduce the words of human beings and the sounds of beasts and the tones of instruments, with no one prompting it to do so, but making it a point of honor not to let anything go unspoken or unimitated. It happened that one of the wealthy citizens of that area was being borne to his grave, to the sound of many trumpets, and since it was a custom that the players halt at that spot, the trumpeters played there a long time to praise and requests for more. The jay after that day remained voiceless and speechless, not giving forth a sound even for the needs of life. This silence was an even greater wonder to those who had previously admired its utterances as they passed by the spot. There were suspicions of poisoning by others who practiced the same art [of bird training], but most inferred that the trumpets had knocked out its hearing. It was neither of these things, but it was restraint, it appears, and a withdrawal of its skill of mimicry into itself, as the bird prepared and perfected its voice like a musical instrument. All of a sudden, its voice returned and blazed forth, not any of its usual and customary imitations, but articulations of the trumpet's tunes, with all of their intervals and modulations and rhythms. Thus, as I have stated, self-instruction in animals is a stronger evidence of reason than is ease of learning.

(*On the Cleverness of Animals* 972F–973E)

Animal Language Is Meaningful but Humans Cannot Understand It

Nothing shames us, not the fresh brightness of their skin, not the persuasiveness of their melodious voices, not their cleverness of spirit, not the cleanliness of their lifestyles or the level of understanding in the poor creatures, but for the sake of a little meat we deprive them of life, of the light of the sun, of the lifetime into which they were born and come into existence. And too we believe that their utterances and squeaks are inarticulate sounds and not supplications and entreaties and requests for justice on the part of each one that says, "I do not beg for consideration in the case of need but rather in the case of outrageous conduct: kill me to eat, but not so that you may eat more elaborately."

(De esu carnium [On the Eating of Flesh] 994E)

Sextus Empiricus

Little is known of the life of the Sextus who is author of the *Outlines of Pyrrhonism* excerpted below. He is believed to have lived late in the second century CE, and his epithet Empiricus suggests that he was a physician of the so-called Empiric school which was philosophically allied with the Skeptics. Pyrrhon of Elis (*c*.365–275 BCE), named in the title of Sextus' treatise, was the founder of Greek Skepticism. Just as the Skeptics questioned our ability to know anything because we cannot trust our senses or any other source of knowledge, so the Empirics denied the possibility of absolute knowledge about the human body and held that direct observation of the patient is the most reliable source of medical information, while speculation about the nature of the human body is ultimately pointless because nature is incomprehensible.

Sextus' rather extensive discussion of the two types of *logoi* is directed against philosophers whom he designates as "dogmatics" (*dogmatikoi*) – that is, the Stoics, who were identified in later Greek philosophy as those thinkers who most strenuously denied reason to non-human animals, and one may suspect that Sextus' vigorous argument for rationality in animals, manifested in meaningful language, represents not so much a deep interest in the ancient debate on the nature of animalkind as an attempt to challenge the doctrinaire philosophical approach of the Stoics. Specifically anti-Stoic elements in Sextus' exposition include his attribution of both types of *logos* to non-human animals; his assertion that the intellectual capacities of animals enable them to distinguish the useful from the harmful; and his concession of "virtues" (*aretai*) and skills to non-human animals that allow them to navigate their lives successfully. A specifically Skeptic argument that underlies Sextus' exposition and that is touched upon at the outset of his argument, is the doctrine that animal species apprehend the pleasurable and the painful in a manner different from that of human beings, so that humans cannot be certain that their impressions are any less valid than are those of human beings (this argument is set forth in Diogenes Laertius' life of Pyrrho [*Lives of the Philosophers* IX. 79]).

Animals Possess Two Types of "Reason" (logos)

To heap on yet more arguments, we compare the so-called irrational animals with human beings with regard to their sensory impressions (*phantasian*) (we do not reject some ridicule of the conceited and bragging dogmatists after our own vigorous arguments). Members of our own sect are wont to compare the greater number of irrational animals with mankind, but because the sophistical dogmatists maintain that the comparison is unequal, we will tease them a bit further and base our argument upon one animal alone, the dog, if you please, that animal reckoned the most worthless of all. In fact we shall find that the animals of which we are speaking are not our inferiors with regard to their sensory impressions.

The dogmatists agree that this animal excels us with regard to sensation, for it apprehends more than we do by its sense of smell, tracking down by this sense beasts that it does not see, observing them with its eyes more quickly than we do and hearing them acutely. Let us, therefore, turn to its reasoning ability. One type of this is internal (*endiathetos*) and the other externally expressed (*prophorikos*). Let us look first at the internal. Now, according to those dogmatists with whom we are at present most occupied, namely those of the Stoa, the internal reason is supposed to concern itself with the following: the choice of those things that are akin and the avoidance of those things that are alien; the knowledge of the skills involved in this endeavor; and the apprehension of the virtues proper to one's own nature and to the passions.

Now the dog, the animal upon which we are basing our argument by way of example, makes a choice of those things which are akin to it and avoids the dangerous, since it pursues its food but cowers from a raised whip. So too it possesses a skill that provides those things which are akin to it, namely hunting, and it is not without virtue. If justice consists in giving each his due, the dog, in fawning over those familiar to it and those who treat it well and being on guard against those not related to it and who cause it harm, is not without justice. ...

Now, it is clear, if we have selected as the basis of our argument that animal which chooses those things akin to it and flees those things that cause it trouble, and has a capacity for providing itself with that which is akin to it, and can apprehend and assuage its own sufferings, and is not without virtue, these being the properties in which the perfection of internal reason resides, we have selected the dog as our perfect example. It seems to me that this is why some philosophers call themselves by the name of "Dog."

With regard to external reason, we do not need to inquire at the moment, for even some of the dogmatists have rejected this as contrary to the acquisition of virtue, in pursuit of which they would keep silent during their lessons. Besides that, if a person were, for example, silent, no one would say that he was therefore irrational. But leaving these matters, we observe that animals, about which we are speaking, give forth humanlike sounds, including jays and such others. Even if we do not understand the sounds of the so-called irrational animals, it is not at all unlikely that they are using language though we do not understand it, for when we hear the speech of barbarians, we do not understand it but suppose it uniformly meaningless. We hear dogs giving forth one sound when they are warding off enemies and another when they are howling, and yet another when beaten and still another when they are fawning. Thus if one were to look closely at the matter, one would note a great variety of utterances in this and other sorts of animals in differing situations, so that it could readily be said, judging from these circumstances, that the so-called irrational animals have a share of external reason. If they are inferior to humans neither in the sharpness of their perceptions nor in internal reason, nor, to go further, in external reason, they should then be no less trusted than we in respect to their sensory impressions (*phantasias*).

(Hypotyposes [Outlines of Pyrrhonism] I. 62–67, 72–76)

Porphyry

The third book of Porphyry's treatise *De abstinentia* (*On Abstinence from Animal Flesh*) consists of a lengthy defense of the position that, in contradistinction to the view of the Stoics, animals are entitled to just treatment at the hands of human beings. In the opening paragraph of Book III, Porphyry had observed that the Stoics maintain that humans owe just treatment solely to beings that are, unlike animals, rational, so that, in their opinion, humans can have no obligations toward other animal species. In his third book, Porphyry seeks to prove that non-human animals are in fact creatures that can be described as "having a share" (*metocha*, III. 3) of reason. Porphyry's adjective here is related to the verb that Plutarch had used near the outset of his treatise *De sollertia animalium* (*On the Cleverness of Animals*) to indicate his belief that non-human animals "share in" (*metechein*, 960A) reason.

At the outset of our passage, Porphyry makes clear that his comments are directed against the Stoics. Their doctrine of the two kinds of *logos* is prominent in his exposition, and other evidences of Stoic technical vocabulary can be identified as well. He observes, for example, that the Stoics denied "correct reason" (*orthou logou*, III. 2) not only to animals but also to the vast majority of human beings since, in Stoic teaching, only a very few humans have attained to true reason, while others, even those "striving" (*prokoptontes*, III. 2) toward such perfection, are still bad. The notion of moral striving is frequently encountered in Stoic sources, and Porphyry hints here as well at the Stoic view that there is no middle ground between vice and virtue, a position that Diogenes Laertius, in the course of his life of Zeno (VII. 127), attributes to Stoic moralists.

Porphyry joins Plutarch and Sextus in arguing that humans are misguided in supposing that the utterances of animals are without meaning simply because we cannot understand them, but whereas Sextus was content to observe that humans conclude that the utterances of barbarians are without meaning, Porphyry singles out the Indians, Scythians, Thracians and Syrians as peoples whose utterances are judged by Greek speakers to be without meaning because they cannot understand them. Porphyry goes a step further, in his discussion of the vocalizations of birds, than had either Plutarch or Sextus, in claiming that some fortunate human beings, in particular seers, of whom he singles out Tiresias and Melampous, were granted the ability to understand the language of birds as a gift from the gods. Melampous on one occasion buried a snake and then raised its surviving offspring, who rewarded his kindness by licking his ears and instilling into him the ability to understand the language of all animals. Tiresias was granted the ability to understand the language of animals in recompense for his being struck blind.

Both Types of "Reason" (logos) Exist in Animals

According to the Stoics, there are two types of "reason" (*logou*), the "internal" (*endi-athetou*) and the other, "uttered (*prophorikou*) reason," and too they state that there is perfected reason and faulty reason. It is proper to inquire which of these is lacking in animals: is it only correct reason and not reason in its entirety? Is it reason outright, both the inward and that which issues outward? They seem to charge animals with total deprivation of both varieties of reason, not merely the correct reason, for in [the latter case], animals would not be irrational but rather rational, just as are almost all human beings, according to the Stoics. One or two persons have been born wise, the

Stoics assert, persons in whom alone reason is correct, but all others are bad, even if some are making progress while others have an abundance of baseness in them, though all are in any case possessed of reason. Because they are led along by self-love, [the Stoics] declare that all animals are irrational, one after the other, since they desire to declare that this complete absence of reason stems from their irrationality. And yet, to speak the truth, "reason" (*logos*) is observed in absolutely all animals, with the foundations for its perfection [existing] in many of them.

Now then, since "reason" is twofold, the one [entailed] in utterance and the other in the arrangement [of thought], let us begin with the uttered sort, that type put in order by the voice. If uttered reason is the voice signifying through the tongue those things experienced inwardly and in the soul (this is the most common definition and one not dependant upon any philosophical sect but reflecting solely the concept of "reason"), what in this definition is absent from the utterances of animals? Why has an animal not first thought about what it experiences before it says what it is going to say? I mean by "thought" that which is silently spoken in the soul. Now since that which is spoken by the tongue, however it is given voice, whether in a foreign language or in Greek, or in the speech of dogs or cattle, is "reason," animals possessed of a voice have a share [in reason], with human beings speaking according to human custom and animals according to the customs that each species has been granted by the gods and by nature. If we do not understand them, what of it? Greeks do not understand the Indians, and those brought up in the Attic dialect do not understand the language of the Scythians or of the Thracians or of the Syrians. The sounds that they make appear to others like the squawk of cranes, but the language of each of those peoples can be written down for others of their people and is articulate, just as ours is to us. But for us, the language of the Syrians or of the Persians is unable to be written down and remains inarticulate, just as the language of animals is inarticulate to all humans. For so do we apprehend merely noise and sound, since we are unable to understand the conversation of, for example, the Scythians, and they seem to us to give off confused cries and to make no sense, employing one sound that is longer or shorter, though the conversion of the sound to shape meaning is not at all evident [to us] although their utterance is readily comprehended and capable of expressing many variations as is ours to us.

Likewise in the case of animals, understanding comes to them according to their individual species though what we hear is only noise devoid of meaning because no one who has learned our language has instructed us, using our own language, on how to understand the meaning of what is said by the animals. And yet if we ought to believe the ancients and those in our own and our fathers' time, there are those who are said to have listened to and understood the speech of animals, like Melampous and Tiresias and suchlike among the ancients and not long ago Apollonius of Tyana, of whom it is said that while his companions were present and a swallow happened to appear and speak, he said that the swallow informed the other swallows that an ass had fallen in front of the city while carrying a load of grain, and that the load had spilled to the ground when the animal carrying it had fallen. A certain friend of mine told me that he was fortunate enough to possess a household slave who understood the language of birds, and who said that their speech was completely prophetic and warned of things that would shortly transpire, but my friend said that the slave's understanding was taken away because his mother, fearing that he would be sent as a gift to the emperor, urinated in his ears while he slept.

But let us pass by these tales because of our innate sense of disbelief, though I think that no one is unaware that some races even nowadays have a kind of natural bent for understanding the speech of some animals. Arabs listen to ravens and the Etruscans to eagles, and we would probably all understand all animals if a snake cleansed our ears. Certainly, in any case, the varied and dissimilar nature of their utterances makes it clear that they have meaning. They sound in one way when they are afraid, and in another when they are calling out, and in yet another way when they are asking for food, and in still another when they are showing affection, and in another altogether when they are challenging another to battle. So great is the difference that the variation is hard to observe even for those who have devoted their lives to observing such things. Augurs, who have marked the differences in the speech of ravens and crows up to a point, have left the rest as not easily grasped by humans. But when they speak things that are clear and intelligible to one another, even if those things are not comprehensible to all of us, and when they seem to imitate us and to have learned the Greek tongue and to understand their owners, who would be so reckless as not to agree that they are possessed of reason, just because he does not understand what they say?

(On Abstinence from Animal Flesh III. 2–4)

Suggestions for Further Reading

Diogenes Laertius

Heath, John, *The Talking Greeks: Speech, Animals and the Other in Homer, Aeschylus, and Plato* (Cambridge: Cambridge University Press, 2005). Heath demonstrates that, as the Greeks sought to identify factors that helped to differentiate humans from other animals, they isolated speech as that capacity which allows humans to avoid behaving like animals. He argues that the Greek notion that animals are speechless antedates the notion that they are irrational.

Mühl, "Der λόγος ἐνδιάθετος und προφορικός von der älteren Stoa bis zur Synode von Sirmium."

Newmyer, Stephen T., "The Human Soul and the Animal Soul: Stoic Theory and Its Survival in Contractualist Ethics," in Annetta Alexandridis, Markus Wild and Lorenz Winkler-Horaček, eds, *Mensch und Tier in der Antike: Grenzziehung und Grenzüberschreitung* (Wiesbaden: Reichert Verlag, 2008) 71–80. This study examines the debt of Contractualism to Stoic theory on the nature of the animal soul and its relation to animal intellect and language.

Sorabji, *Animal Minds and Human Morals* 80–86. Sorabji here offers a helpful overview of Greek ideas on animal speech and of modern scientific thought on the topic.

Tabarroni, Andrea, "On Articulation and Animal Language in Ancient Linguistic Theory," *Versus* 50/51 (1988) 103–121. Tracing medieval concepts of the articulation of the voice, Tabarroni discusses their debt to Greek ideas on whether animal utterances are meaningful and constitute language.

Aristotle

Dierauer, *Tier und Mensch* 126–128. Dierauer here offers helpful analysis of Aristotle's complex pronouncements on animal and human vocalizations, with references to various treatises of the philosopher.

Philo of Alexandria

Terian, *Philonis Alexandrini de Animalibus* 203–204. Terian's commentary on paragraph 98 provides references to other discussions of the two types of *logos* in the works of Philo, with extensive references.

Plutarch

Newmyer, Stephen T., "Speaking of Beasts: the Stoics and Plutarch on Animal Reason and the Modern Case against Animals," *QUCC* 63, 3 (1999) 99–110. This study examines Plutarch's arguments for rationality in animals as this is demonstrated in the language of birds, and discusses the debt of Contractualism to Stoic theory on animal vocalizations.

Sextus Empiricus

Dierauer, *Tier und Mensch* 256–258, 268–269. Dierauer provides a helpful analysis of Sextus' comments on reason in animals.

Porphyry

Sorabji, *Animal Minds and Human Morals* 80–86. Sorabji provides a penetrating analysis of ancient pronouncements on the language of animals, with particular reference to Porphyry's discussion of the topic.

Part II

HUMAN–ANIMAL RELATIONS

4

ANIMALS AS MORAL BEINGS

1. Justice toward Animals

The preoccupation of ancient philosophers and naturalists with the question of whether non-human animals possess reason was no matter of idle speculation but had enormous practical implications for the lives of humans, not to mention those of non-human animals. Since antiquity, claims that humans stand alone in possessing reason have been used as the basis for an assertion of human moral superiority and as a justification for excluding other animal species from human moral concern. The underlying assumption of much speculation on animal intellect was that rationality in itself conferred moral considerability upon those who possessed it. The Stoics took up Aristotle's denial of reason (*logos, logismos*) to animals and gave his essentially biological view of animal intellect a distinctly moral dimension. This is observable in the Stoic doctrine of *oikeiōsis*, "kinship, relationship, belonging," examined in Part I of this volume. Stoicism, in particular among ancient schools, sought to emphasize the "differentness" of irrational animals vis-à-vis their rational human counterparts, while figures such as Plutarch and Porphyry attempted to demonstrate that rationality in animals was not a matter of "all or nothing," but rather one of degree. If, as the Stoics argued, animals are utterly unlike human beings, humans can have no obligation to refrain from using them in any manner that benefits humans.

If it emerged, on the other hand, that animals are, as Plutarch and Porphyry argued, possessed of some degree of rationality, and if reason-possession was the criterion that granted moral considerability to animals, as the Stoics demanded, one is then compelled to ask: are animals the sorts of beings that can stand in a relationship with human beings that would be called "justice," and what would that term mean when applied to interspecies relations? As the passages excerpted below make clear, this issue was debated as hotly as that of whether animals are rational. Some thinkers even asked whether animals might themselves have a conception of justice that they applied in their own relations with other animals and even with human beings.

In the passage below, Diogenes Laertius illustrates the Stoic denial of justice toward animals based on their lack of rationality and their consequent differentness from human beings. The doctrine of *oikeiōsis* serves as the basis for Chrysippus' denial of justice to animals here. Porphyry (*On Abstinence from Animal Flesh* III. 20) reports that Chrysippus also taught that animals were created by the gods specifically for the use of man, and that pigs were born expressly to be slaughtered. Their souls, the Stoic taught, were merely a preservative, like salt, which improves their flavor when humans ate the pigs.

Diogenes Laertius

Chrysippus Says Justice toward Animals Is Impossible

Moreover, it is their teaching that no justice exists between humans and other animals because of their dissimilarity. So Chrysippus says in the first book of his *On Justice* and Posidonius in the first book of his *On Duty*.

(***Lives of the Philosophers*** VII. 129 [from the life of Zeno the Stoic])

Aristotle

As with Chrysippus, Aristotle's denial in the passage below from his *Nicomachean Ethics* of the possibility of a relationship of justice between humans and non-human animals rests on an assertion of a lack of anything in common (*koinon*) between the species. His denial here is in keeping with his claim (*Politics* 1256b15–23; translated on p. 27), that animals are made for man's use, a view which presupposes the absence of any moral ties between the species, but his formulation of the question of justice is more sweeping in the present passage. Both friendship and justice are declared to be impossible, not only between humans and animals but between persons of unequal social and political station. A ruler is declared unable to share friendship or justice with those he rules, again because they have nothing in common (*koinon*).

In the *Politics*, Aristotle links a sense of justice with the possession of language on the principle that those who seek justice must be capable of articulating the concept of the just and the unjust through meaningful speech. Animal utterances are limited to the conveyance of the notions of the painful and the pleasurable (on animal speech, see pp. 59–69). The inability of animals to convey through speech a concept of the just and the unjust prevents them from forming a state, in which appreciation for the nature of justice is fundamental. Aristotle seems to foreshadow here the idea, prominent in Epicurean ethics (see pp. 28–29), that justice arises from a contract or covenant between those who desire justice and those who must possess articulate speech to express that desire.

Justice toward Animals Is Impossible

In perverted [governments], in the same way that justice cannot advance far, so is there no friendship, and least so in the worst sort [of government], for in a tyranny there is no or very little friendship. In situations in which there is nothing in common between ruler and ruled, there is no friendship, nor justice either. So it is for a workman toward his tool, or the soul toward the body or a master toward his slave. All of these things are benefited by those who use them, but there is no friendship or justice toward inanimate objects. Nor is there toward a horse or an ox or toward a slave as slave, for there is nothing in common between them.

(*Nicomachean Ethics* 1161a30–1161b2)

Speech Articulates Right and Wrong, and Animals have no Speech

As we say, nature does nothing to no end, and man alone of the animals has speech. Now, the voice is the indicator of the painful and the pleasurable, because of which it exists in the other animals as well, for their nature is advanced to the point that they have the sensation of pain and pleasure and signal these to one another. Speech, however, exists to indicate the advantageous and the harmful, and thus likewise the just and the unjust: this is one special characteristic of human beings, in contrast to the other animals, that they alone have perception of the good and the bad and the just and the unjust, as of other things as well, and the common possession of these things creates a household and a state.

(*Politics* 1253a9–18)

Cicero

In the same manner that Cicero's dialogue *De finibus bonorum et malorum* (*On the Ends of Good and Evil*) set forth the views of the Stoic, Epicurean and Academic schools of philosophy on the nature of the highest good (*summum bonum*) in human life (see pp. 41–42), so did his dialogue *De natura deorum* (*On the Nature of the Gods*), composed in 45 BCE, set forth the views of those three schools on the existence of the gods and the nature of the divine. Book II is devoted to an exposition of the Stoic position on these matters, set forth by one Balbus who is otherwise unknown.

In the passage from *On the Nature of the Gods* translated below, Balbus explains how animals fit into the scheme of Stoic theology. His starkly anthropocentric account recalls Aristotle's pronouncement (*Politics* 1256b15–23; see p. 27) that animals exist for the sake of human beings, but, taken as a whole, it is probably more to be interpreted as an elaboration of the Chrysippean view of the place of animals in the scheme of creation, which is detailed in Porphyry (*On Abstinence from Animal Flesh* III. 20; see p. 74), with its assumption that animals are in a sense living commodities existing only to be put to use by human beings. Just as Chrysippus had claimed that pigs live only to be slaughtered and eaten by humans, so Cicero's Balbus asserts that the sheep lives only to await its conversion into clothing for humans.

The specifically Stoic justification for the ungenerous views toward animals that Balbus voices is laid out in the opening sentences of his exposition: the world is the common home or city of gods and men, a circumstance due to their common possession of reason. At issue again is the Stoic doctrine of *oikeiōsis*: gods and men are akin and related because of their shared rationality, while animals, as irrational entities, are necessarily left out of this community.

The same idea of man's justification in using animals as needed emerges in the excerpt below from Cicero's dialogue *On the Ends of Good and Evil*, here specifically linked to the Chrysippean formulation of the idea and expounded in Cicero by Cato the Younger (96–46 BCE), a Roman politician and Stoic adherent of legendary moral rectitude. Here, however, the conversation relates more to the Stoic assertion of a lack of any natural relationship of justice between species based, once again, on the dissimilarity of their intellectual endowments (see also the formulation of this Chrysippean idea in Diogenes Laertius (*Lives of the Philosophers* VII. 129, translated on p. 74).

Animals Are Intended for Man's Use

[BALBUS]:   It remains for me to demonstrate (making an end to my exposition) how all things that human beings use in the world were made and furnished for their sake. To begin with, the world itself was created for the sake of the gods and humans, and the things that it contains were provided and produced for the sake of men. For the world is, so to speak, a common home to gods and men, or a city for both. They alone live by the use of reason and law. Just as we must suppose that the cities of Athens and Sparta were established for the sake of the Athenians and the Spartans, and all things that are in these cities are rightly said to belong to those peoples, so whatever things exist in the whole world must be supposed to belong to the gods and to men. Every revolution of the sun and the moon and of every other celestial body, though these also pertain to the cohesion of the universe, nevertheless provides a spectacle for human beings. There is no sight more eternally satisfying, more beautiful or more demonstrative of reason and skill. By measuring out their courses we know the fullness of the seasons and their differences and changes. If these things are known to human beings alone, we must conclude that they were created for the sake of human beings.

Does it seem that the earth, which is fertile with fruits and various sorts of plants, produces these things for the sake of wild beasts or for human beings? What shall I say of vines and olives, whose very abundant fruits are of no use at all to animals? Animals know nothing of sowing and tilling or of reaping and gathering crops in season or of storing them. This is entirely an occupation and employment of human beings. Just as we must say that lyres and flutes were made for the sake of those who use them, so we must admit that those things which I have mentioned are furnished solely for those who use them. If animals steal away and carry off some of these things, will we say that they were created for the sake of those animals? Nor either do human beings store away grain for the use of mice or ants but rather for their own wives and children and households. Thus, as I have suggested, animals enjoy these products by theft while their masters enjoy them openly and freely. We must therefore acknowledge that this bounty was created for the sake of man, unless perhaps such richness and variety of fruit with its pleasant flavor and appearance causes us to doubt whether nature gave this gift to human beings alone.

However far from the truth it is that such things were produced for the sake of animals too, we must in any case admit that animals themselves were produced for the sake of man. What other uses do sheep have beyond the fact that humans are clothed in their processed and woven wool? They could not have been nourished or raised without the care and tending of human beings, nor have produced anything of value. What do the faithful watchfulness of dogs, and their fawning adulation of their masters and their hostility toward strangers, the incredible keenness of their noses, and their eagerness in the hunt, what do these mean except that they were produced for the convenience of human beings? Why should I mention oxen? Their very backs indicate that they were not shaped for carrying burdens, but their necks were designed to bear the yoke and their powerful and broad shoulders were made for pulling the plough. Since the earth was brought under control with their aid through the breakup of the clods of the soil, no violence was ever shown them in the Golden Age, as the poets say:

Suddenly sprang up a race of men of iron,
Which first dared forge a deadly sword
And tasted the ox it yoked and tamed by hand.
The profit derived from oxen was reckoned so great that it was considered a crime to
    eat their flesh.

(De natura deorum [On the Nature of the Gods] II. 154–159)

Humans Can Use Animals as They See Fit without Injustice

[CATO]:   But just as [the Stoics] believe that the bonds of right exist between human and human, so do they believe that a human has no bond of right with beasts. For Chrysippus [has remarked] admirably that other things were born for the sake of men and the gods, and that moreover they were born for their own fellowship and society, so that humans may use beasts for their own advantage without injustice.

(On the Ends of Good and Evil III. 67)

Plutarch

In the selection below from Plutarch's dialogue *On the Cleverness of Animals*, a treatise which argues that all animals have at least a share of reason (960A; see pp. 17–18), we can isolate a number of arguments and counterarguments that were regularly marshaled by both sides in the ancient debate on whether non-human species can stand in a relation of justice with human beings. Plutarch's interlocutor Soclarus, who defends the Stoic position in the dialogue, makes it clear early on in his comments that the central issue in the debate is the question of rationality in animals, which the Stoics had of course denied to them. To accord reason to animals would have far-reaching and dire consequences for human life, as Soclarus demonstrates. Justice will itself be confounded and human life turned upside down if humans cease to use animals for their own needs. Humans are left in a quandary: if a relation of justice exists between species, we must either commit injustice in putting them to use for our needs, or we must find human life rendered impossible if we leave them undisturbed. Soclarus reveals his Stoic orientation, and the Stoic flow of his argument, in his observation that human life will be forced to the impasse that he foresees, if animals are after all rational, and akin to humans. Once again, the Stoic doctrine of *oikeiōsis* provides a solution for the Stoics: since humans have no natural kinship with animals, in Stoic teaching, humans are released from any possibility of committing injustice toward them because animals are irrational. Soclarus may have in mind here Chrysippus' declaration that no justice can exist between man and other animals because of their "unlikeness" to humans (Diogenes Laertius VII. 129).

At the end of his exposition, Soclarus briefly raises an issue that, while less frequently encountered than the question of human justice toward animals, is not unparalleled: do non-human animals have the capacity to practice justice in their own lives (see pp. 82–86, for this topic). In support of his contention that they do not, Soclarus cites the famous lines of Hesiod (*Works and Days* 277–279) in which the didactic poet maintains that animals were denied a sense of justice (*dikē*) by Zeus, who awarded this solely to human beings.

Autobulus, Plutarch's mouthpiece in *On the Cleverness of Animals*, teases his friend Soclarus that, just as the Epicureans should not be allowed to make assertions that they cannot prove, namely the existence of atoms, so should the Stoics not be allowed to make assertions about the nature of justice without proving them or taking into account the objections of their philosophical opponents. The principal value of Autobulus' rebuttal, however, is its offer of a compromise between the two unpalatable consequences of an admission of the existence of reason in animals that Soclarus has posited. Citing Heraclitus and Empedocles as authorities for the position that humans cannot act entirely justly in their relations with other animals, Autobulus allows that man will act as much in accord with reason as is practicable in human life if he kills only those animals that pose a danger to him while making reasonable use, as in farming, of those animals that are gentle and harmless to man. He touches in passing on the concept of the "just war" that some felt humans could wage against natural predators, a concept discussed by Aristotle (*Politics* 1256b23–26), who maintains that it is just for humans to slay both wild animals and other human beings who are intended by nature to be ruled but who refuse.

Autobulus' exposition concludes with an aspect of the question of justice toward animals that is only infrequently encountered in classical sources, namely the issue of kindness toward animals. Having allowed humans to make use of some animals in a responsible manner, Autobulus sets limits to that use. Not quite demanding a vegetarian lifestyle on the part of human beings, as he would in his treatise *On the Eating of Flesh* (see pp. 105–108), Plutarch here at least allows his mouthpiece to enjoin his fellow humans to refrain from overt cruelty in their treatment of food animals and of wild animals that they encounter in daily life. While the use of animals is not declared to be in itself unjust, the wanton treatment of other species is condemned as abominable.

Kindness toward Animals Does Not Overturn Justice

SOCLARUS: Your conjecture seems correct to me, for the Stoics and the Peripatetics argue in the opposite direction entirely, maintaining that justice could have no other origin, but would be altogether formless and insubstantial, if all animals have a share of reason. For it is then necessarily the case that injustice arises if we do not spare them, or that life becomes impossible and inconceivable if we do not make use of them. In a sense we will live the lives of beasts if we give up the use of beasts. I pass over the innumerable hordes of Nomads and Troglodytes who know no other diet than meat, but it is hard to say what activity on land will be left to us who think that we live in a civilized and benevolent manner, what pursuit on sea or mountain, what adornment of lifestyle, if we learn to behave without injury and with circumspection toward all animals, as we will be obligated to do if they are rational and akin to us. We have therefore no remedy or cure for this dilemma which deprives us either of life or of justice, unless we preserve the ancient limit by which, according to Hesiod, [Zeus], in differentiating the natures of creatures and placing each sort of creature into its own species:

Let fish and beasts and flying birds
Devour each other, since they have no justice in them,
But he gave justice to humans,
so that humans could exercise it toward each other.

It is impossible for us to act unjustly toward those who do not have the capacity to behave justly toward us. Truly, those who have tossed aside this line of reasoning have left no other path, wide or narrow, for justice to enter.

AUTOBULUS: You have spoken this from your heart, my dear friend. We should not allow philosophers, like women in painful childbirth, to hang on themselves a charm for easy delivery, so that they may give birth to justice for us easily and without pain. For they do not allow to Epicurus, in matters of the greatest importance, even the small and trivial phenomenon of a swerve in the atom, to the slightest degree, so that stars and animals and chance could enter in and free will would not perish. But [Epicurus] must demonstrate a thing that is not seen or choose something that is manifest to the senses and not make any arguments concerning justice toward animals unless it is agreed upon by all and unless [the Stoics] make no counterargument. Justice has another path, however, one neither slippery nor steep nor leading through rejected facts, but which, under Plato's guidance, my son and your companion, dear Soclarus, points out to those who do not wish to argue but who are willing to follow and learn. Empedocles and Heraclitus accept as true the proposition that man is not entirely free of injustice when he treats animals thus, lamenting and branding nature as "necessity" and "warfare," a being that contains nothing unmixed or uncorrupted but one brought to fullness of being filled with many injustices. They maintain that even birth itself happens through acts of injustice since the immortal comes together with the mortal, and the creature born is nurtured, contrary to nature, by limbs torn from the one that gave it birth.

Well, these ideas seem excessively violent and bitter, but there exists another, more agreeable argument, one that does not deprive animals of reason but that preserves justice for those who are willing to employ the argument. When the wise men of old introduced this argument, gluttony rose up and, joined with luxury, cast it out and made it disappear, but Pythagoras reintroduced it, teaching us to benefit without committing injustice. For they do not commit injustice who punish and slay those animals that are savage and quite harmful while taming those that are gentle and well-disposed toward human beings, making them our fellow-workers in the tasks for which each was born,

The offspring of horse and ass and the stock of bulls,
which the Prometheus of Aeschylus says he gave to us,
To be like servants and relieve our tasks.

Likewise we use dogs when we are keeping watch, and we tend herds of goats and sheep that we milk and shear. Life is not taken away or destroyed for men if they do not have platters of fish or goose liver pâté and do not slaughter cattle and goat kids for their banquets or do not, when lounging at the theater or entertaining themselves at the hunt, force animals to make shows of courage against their will and to put up a fight, and destroy others that do not by their nature defend themselves. I think that the person who engages in happy sport should do so with companions who are likewise at play, and that sport should not be as Bion describes it, saying that children amuse themselves by throwing stones at frogs, but the frogs are not playing but in fact dying. So too in the case of hunting and fishing, men kill animals and enjoy their sufferings, taking from them their whelps and nestlings in a pitiful manner. Thus those persons who make use of animals do not commit injustice, but rather they are unjust who use them in a cruel and contemptuous and savage manner.

(On the Cleverness of Animals 963F–965B)

Porphyry

The third book of Porphyry's treatise *De abstinentia* (*On Abstinence from Animal Flesh*) argues that human beings have a debt of justice toward other species because, despite Stoic denials, animals are endowed with rationality which he terms "incomplete, but not totally absent," which renders them akin (*oikeioi*) to human beings. They possess, he maintains, both *logos endiathetos* and *logos prophorikos*, the latter contributing to a complex language which humans cannot comprehend, as well as emotions (*pathē*) and, as he maintains in the excerpt below, a sense of justice arising from their participation in reason. The overall shape of Porphyry's argument here, that humans owe justice to other creatures that are rational and therefore partake of that kinship and relationship (*oikeiōsis*) upon which the Stoics predicated inclusion in the sphere of human moral concern, recalls Plutarch's case for justice toward animals (see pp. 77–80), which is not surprising since substantial portions of Porphyry's third book (III. 20. 7–III. 24. 5) are copied almost word for word from Plutarch's treatise *On the Cleverness of Animals* (959E–963F). Even the rather infrequently encountered argument that animals have themselves a sense of justice which they exercise toward each other (see also pp. 82–86), with which the excerpt opens, suggests Plutarchan influence, for the earlier author had argued that the well-regulated social lives of animals and the love that they bear toward their offspring suggest a sense of justice in them (*On the Cleverness of Animals* 962A).

The Rational Souls of Animals Demand Animals Be Treated with Justice

Who is unaware that animals living in groups observe justice toward one another? Every ant, every bee does so, as do creatures like these. Who does not know of the chastity of the wood-pigeon toward her mate? If she has been seduced, she destroys the seducer if he is caught. Who does not know of the justice of storks toward their parents? In each animal there exists some individual virtue to which it is naturally disposed, but neither nature nor the strength of that virtue takes away their reason. This is the fact that one must refute if the acts of virtue are deemed to be not in line with rational ability. If we do not understand how these things are done because we cannot enter into their reasoning process, we shall not therefore accuse them of irrationality. No one is capable either of entering into the mind of god, but based on the actions of the sun we agree with those who pronounce god to be intellectual and rational.

One might be amazed at those who derive justice from reason and say that animals that do not live in the company of humans are wild and unjust, but still they do not extend justice to those animals that do live in our company. Just as life is obliterated for humans if this company is taken away, so too for animals. Birds and dogs and many quadrupeds including goats, horses, sheep, donkeys and mules perish if deprived of human company. Nature that created them made them need humans and humans need them as well, constructing in them an innate justice toward us as in us toward them. If certain animals are savage toward humans, that is not to be wondered at. Aristotle was correct to remark that if all animals had sufficient food to eat, they would not behave savagely toward each other or toward humans, for it is because of food, a necessary and cheap commodity, that hatreds and friendships arise in them, as well as because of territorial disputes. Now if humans were forced into exactly these difficulties, how much more savage would they be than those creatures deemed to be savage? War and famine illustrate this, since humans do not refrain from eating one another. Even without war and famine humans eat tame animals that dwell among them. ...

From these arguments and others that we will mention in turn in reviewing the writings of the ancients, it is clear that animals are rational, their rationality being, in many cases, incomplete, but not totally absent. If then justice exists toward rational beings, as our opponents maintain, why would justice not be owed to animals by us humans?

(On Abstinence from Animal Flesh III. 11–12, 18)

Suggestions for Further Reading

Diogenes Laertius on Chrysippus

Sorabji, *Animal Minds and Human Morals* 124–126, 142–143. After explicating the Stoic doctrine of *oikeiōsis*, including a discussion of Chrysippus' denial of reason to animals (124–126), Sorabji attempts (142–143) to define the Stoic understanding of "justice" as consisting more of a recognition of that which is appropriate than a distribution of that which is due to others.

Aristotle

Vegetti, Mario, "Figure dell' Animale in Aristotele." The author argues that Aristotle's tendency to regard animals as perpetual babies and as slaves rendered him incapable of conceiving that animals could pursue any avenue of upright conduct that humans pursue.

Cicero

Reydams-Schils, Gretchen, "Human Bonding and *Oikeiōsis* in Roman Stoicism." The author demonstrates that the Roman emphasis on human ties with other humans exercised a powerful influence upon the Roman brand of Stoicism, not least in its understanding of Stoic kinship theory.

Plutarch

Barigazzi, Adelmo, "Implicanze nella Polemica Plutarchea sulla Psicologia degli Animali." This article contains a detailed analysis of Stoic arguments against according justice to animals and a discussion of Plutarch's compromise solution that allows limited human use of other species.

Becchi, Francesco, "Istinto e Intelligenza negli Scritti Zoopsicologici di Plutarco." Becchi isolates the philosophical schools that contributed to the ancient debate concerning the possibility of according justice to animals, and he demonstrates Plutarch's use of material from these schools.

Newmyer, Stephen T., "Plutarch on Justice toward Animals: Ancient Insights on a Modern Debate," *Scholia: Natal Studies in Classical Antiquity* 1 (1992) 38–54. This study examines Plutarch's views on the possibility of justice toward animals as his arguments anticipate those of modern animal rights activists on the subject of justice.

Porphyry

Pérez-Paoli, Ubaldo, "Porphyrios' Gedanken zur Gerechtigkeit gegenüber den Tieren." The author traces Theophrastean and Academic elements in Porphyry's arguments for justice toward animals.

2. Justice from Animals

Hesiod

The verses below from the didactic poem *Works and Days*, a loosely organized treatise on farming with observations on practical morality composed by the Boeotian farmer Hesiod (8th century BCE?), constitute the earliest extant Greek attempt to differentiate human beings from other animals on philosophical grounds, and may be considered to be the first Greek example of the "man alone of animals" commonplace. Cited by Plutarch in his discussion of justice toward animals (*On the Cleverness of Animals* 964B; see pp. 78–80), Hesiod addresses these verses to his dishonest brother Perses who had cheated him of some of their father's estate, and he argues that humans, unlike animals, have been given an understanding of justice, which the gods denied to other species. One cannot therefore expect animals to behave with restraint in their relations with other animals, as the gods expect humans to do.

Hesiod's verses are valuable not so much for their insight into early Greek views on man's debt of justice toward other species as for their early articulation of the view, less frequently encountered in ancient literature, that animals themselves have no conception of justice. This embryonic idea in Hesiod would be developed by later Greek philosophers, including the Stoics, to argue that humans are not obligated to act justly toward creatures that cannot act justly in return.

Zeus Did Not Give Animals a Sense of Justice

O Perses, ponder this in your mind: pay heed to justice now and forget violence, for Zeus son of Kronos has established this as a norm for human beings, that fish and wild beasts and winged birds should eat one another since there is no justice in them; but he gave justice to humans, which is the best thing of all by far.

(*Works and Days* 274–280)

Democritus

Although the Presocratic philosopher Democritus of Abdera in Thrace (*c*.460–357 BCE) is remembered primarily for championing an atomistic explanation of the universe and for being thus a source for later Epicureanism, extant fragments of his works and testimonia relating to his teachings suggest that he had some intriguing things to say on the possibility of an ethical relationship between humans and other species. In the fragments below, the philosopher argues that animals may act contrary to justice (*para dikēn*) in a manner that suggests an intention to do so on the part of the animals (*thelonta adikein*). Consequently, humans who kill such animals commit no act of injustice (*athōios ho kteinōn*) toward them. While Democritus does not raise the possibility that animals possess a sense of justice that they apply in their relations with fellow-animals, he does suggest that animals bear responsibility for their actions and are therefore subject to human justice. Nor are animals the only ones to fall under Democritus' view of justice, which calls for the slaying of all creatures that act contrary to human justice.

Although the Stoics would have approved of Democritus' apparent support of the idea that the interests of humans take precedence over those of non-human species, he argues for the possibility of voluntary action on the part of animals, which the Stoics rejected on the grounds that animals are irrational. In Stoic teaching, animals, because of their intellectual limitations, cannot be held responsible for their actions, a position that Democritus opposes here.

Animals May Act Contrary to Justice

With regard to certain animals, the rule on killing them or not is as follows: he who kills those that commit injustice and those that seek to be unjust [should be] free of blame, and doing so contributes more to well-being than not doing so.

One must by all means kill all creatures that cause harm contrary to justice. And he who does so will have a greater share of cheerfulness and justice and bravery and property in every organized society.

("Democritus," DK 257–258)

Cicero

Cicero's treatise *De officiis* (*On Duties*), the last of the orator's philosophical works, was published in 44 BCE. In its three books, cast in the form of an extended letter to his son, he offers an analysis of the four cardinal ancient virtues – wisdom, justice, courage and temperance – and attempts to instruct the reader on how honorable behavior can be applied in real-life situations. Conflict between honor and expediency is shown to be merely an illusion. The first two books of the work were based, according to Cicero, on a treatise by the Stoic Panaetius (*c*.185–109 BCE) called *On Duty*, a work now lost, while the third book was based on the thought of the Stoic Posidonius (*c*.135–51 BCE). Given his reliance on Stoic sources, it is not surprising that Cicero builds a case against a sense of justice in non-human species that relies heavily on the Stoic denial of reason and thus of articulate language to animals and that has as its theoretical basis the Stoic doctrine of *oikeiōsis*, the bond or sense of belonging that humans share with other humans founded on their common possession of reason and speech and their ability to communicate their interests to one another. Cicero's use of such phrases as "community and human society" (*communitatis et societatis humanae*), "universal kinship of the human race" (*universi generis humani societate*) and "bonding agent" (*vinculum*), all suggest that Cicero has Stoic kinship theory in mind.

Animals Have No Sense of Justice

But it appears that we must first recall what things in nature constitute the foundations of community and human society; the first principle is observable in the universal kinship of the human race. The bonding agent of that kinship is reason and speech, which unites humans in the actions of teaching, learning, communicating, debating and adjudicating, and links them in a certain natural bond. In no respect are we further away from the nature of wild beasts, in which we often say that there is bravery, as in the case of horses and lions, but we do not say that there exist justice, fairness or goodness in them, for they are without reason and speech.

(*De officiis* [*On Duties*] I. 50)

Philo of Alexandria

In paragraphs 61 and 64 from Philo's dialogue *On Animals*, the author's nephew Alexander, defender of rationality in animals, cites examples of just behavior in animals that were stereotypic in ancient discussions of animal intellect. Alexander's claim that storks feed their parents, for example, recurs in Aristotle (*History of Animals* 615b23–24), Aelian (*Nature of Animals* III. 23) and Plutarch (*On the Cleverness of Animals* 962E). Alexander draws the conclusion from this behavior that such apparent evidence of a sense of justice in the birds suggests the presence of a degree of reason. The very propensity of animals to travel in herds or flocks suggests some sense of justice in animals since they are willing to follow the leaders that they have selected. In the final sentence of paragraph 64, Alexander alludes to the ancient belief, discussed as well by Plutarch (*On the Cleverness of Animals* 975A) and Aelian (*Nature of Animals* VII. 7), that the formations of birds have prophetic significance.

Philo's refutation of Alexander's arguments shows Stoic inspiration since he maintains that the actions of storks are involuntary and cannot therefore be counted as instances of just behavior any more than of unjust behavior. According to the Stoics, animals cannot give or withhold assent from their own actions, because involuntary actions require the operation of reason, and animals are, in Stoic teaching, irrational, a Stoic position to which Philo alludes in the final sentence of paragraph 96. In the same way, Philo argues, no one blames a child for its actions because it is still pre-rational, although, unlike non-human animals, the human child will eventually attain rationality.

Do Animals Have a Sense of Justice?

Among the birds the stork exhibits supreme justice by feeding its parents in return. As soon as it begins to fly, it sets no other task above that of reciprocating the favors of those that fostered it. It is possible that some of the terrestrial animals behave like it. But since we cannot tell all of their instincts and can never see nor ascertain them, we ought to believe what the witnesses have revealed about these things we have not seen. For it is right that the universe should be composed not of some only of its parts but of them all. Moreover that part in which justice and injustice are found is preeminently endowed with reason, since both pertain to reason, which, just as it is imparted to men, should likewise be imparted to those animals cited. The storks that feed their parents and give due consideration to the old, also punish. The pinna-guards, noted for sharing their food together with the pinnae, deal fairly with the injurious and the adverse, lest those named should be done away with. As for the bees, swarms of workers consider the drones detrimental to honeycombs so they kill them. For indeed as Hesiod has said, they reap the toil of others into their own bellies.

(On Animals 61)

Animals, no less than men, show great – if not better – demonstrations of equality and justice. The leaders they appoint and the offices to which they designate them are never ignored. They follow with all willingness those whom they choose to be leaders. Eyes ascertain the veracity of what is said. A young bull leads herds of cattle, a he-goat flocks of goats, and a ram flocks of sheep. An extremely large number of animals follow as irregular troops raised by royal commissioners. This sense of following must be divinely imbued.

(On Animals 64)

Furthermore if the stork does not feed its parents in return, it could not be accused of injustice, even though it would appear to be an act of injustice, for it is involuntary. Nor are drones deemed transgressors when they waste the labor of the bees; they do not do this voluntarily but rather are prompted by the desire for food. Have you not noticed that no one ever blames a little child for anything he does, since he has not yet attained to an accountable age? Although an infant is immature, he is a rational man by nature, having newly received the seeds of wisdom, which, though not yet developed, will soon mature. Throughout the duration of his growth, the seminal powers spread rapidly like sparks in a forest, fanned by a breeze or wind. But the souls of other creatures do not have the fount of wisdom. They are destitute of the reasoning faculty.

(On Animals 96)

Suggestions for Further Reading

Hesiod

Dierauer, *Tier und Mensch* 15–18. Dierauer offers a valuable appreciation of Hesiod's denial of justice to animals as it developed in the course of subsequent classical speculation on animals, emphasizing Hesiod's position as the first Greek to distinguish humans from other animals rather than from gods.

Democritus

Cole, Thomas, *Democritus and the Sources of Greek Anthropology* (Cleveland: Press of Western Reserve University, 1967). This classic text provides useful discussion of Democritus' pronouncements on the lack of rational faculties in animals and on man's justly adversarial stance toward hostile animal species.

Cicero

Reydams-Schils, "Human Bonding and *Oikeiōsis* in Roman Stoicism."

Philo of Alexandria

Terian, *Philonis Alexandrini de Animalibus* 173–175, 177–178, 201–202. Terian's commentaries on paragraphs 61, 64 and 96 of Philo's *On Animals* supply references to classical texts relating to justice and animals, as well as to discussions of this topic in Philo's other works.

5

ANIMALS AS OFFERINGS: HUNTING AND SACRIFICE

1. Plato

Greco-Roman attitudes toward hunting were complex and ambivalent, and suggest that the practice involved a cluster of both practical and symbolic meanings in classical society. Viewed not merely as a means of procuring food, hunting was seen by some ancient writers as evidence of the triumph of human reason and ingenuity over creatures considered either inferior to humans or clever enough to be worthy adversaries that put humans to the test and brought out the best in them as they sought to outwit and outmaneuver their beastly foe. Hence expressions of guilt at the necessity of depriving innocent creatures of their lives so that humans can sustain their own are found alongside assertions that hunting provides humans with innocent amusement and expressions of triumph at the removal of beasts intent upon obliterating the human race. This latter notion contributed to the view, advanced, for example, in Aristotle (*Politics* 1256b23–26), that human beings wage a "just war" against wild nature. Hunting becomes, in this interpretation, almost a matter of self-defense on the part of human beings. On the other hand, the Greeks maintained a certain wariness in their approach to hunting because it was from earliest times considered the pastime of the gods who functioned at the same time as protectors of wild species. Overhunting and wanton cruelty in the practice might draw down the fury of the gods, in particular of Artemis, goddess of the hunt and patroness of wild nature.

The seventh book of Plato's final dialogue, *Nomoi* (*Laws*), deals with the education of the young, and offers remarks on the practice of hunting that reflect both enthusiasm for the practice and reservations at its potential excesses. The chief interlocutor in the treatise, called simply "an Athenian," prefaces the remarks excerpted below with the observation that hunting deserves praise and censure in that it renders the souls of young persons both better and worse (*Laws* 823d). Fishing, for example, is called an unworthy pursuit since nets and traps do the hunter's work for him, while snaring birds is beneath the dignity of a free man. Only hunting with dogs and horses, in which the hunter takes an active part, is truly worthy of a free man (*Laws* 824b).

Laws on Hunting

[ATHENIAN:]   "Let this discussion then serve as our praise and censure on this subject
overall. The law shall be worded thus: 'Let no person hinder these truly sacred hunters from hunting wherever and however they might wish, but let no one ever allow the
night-hunter who relies on nets and snares to hunt anywhere. Let no one hinder the
bird-catcher from hunting in fallow fields and mountains, but let him who encounters
this hunter in cultivated fields or sacred lands drive him off. Let the fisherman be
permitted to hunt in all waters excepting refuges and sacred rivers and marshes and
lakes, provided he uses no muddying juices.' Now then, we can say that we have
completed our laws concerning hunting."
KLEINIAS: "You might well say so."

(*Laws* 824b–c)

2. Plutarch

Plutarch's dialogue *De sollertia animalium* (*On the Cleverness of Animals*) opens with
discussion of an "encomium on hunting" that was read aloud to the participants
in the dialogue on the previous day. Some scholars have surmised that this may
be an allusion to Plutarch's own treatise *On Hunting*, but since that work is lost,
no conclusion can be drawn on this. While Plutarch argues in *On the Cleverness of
Animals* for the presence of some degree of reason in animals, and offers a passionate
defense of the vegetarian lifestyle in his work *On the Eating of Flesh* (see pp. 105–108),
Plutarch's attitude toward hunting may after all have been conflicted if indeed he
authored an "encomium" on the pursuit. It is noteworthy that both Autobulus,
whom Plutarch uses in *On the Cleverness of Animals* to advance ideas with which he
was himself sympathetic, and Soclarus, who espouses Stoic ideas to which Plutarch
was opposed, advance respectful and even cautiously favorable attitudes toward
hunting in the passage below. Arguments for and against the practice that would
become commonplaces in ancient discussions of hunting are encountered: the idea
that hunting offers human beings innocent pleasure and a worthy battle of wits
against clever adversaries is countered by the observation that hunting tends to
blunt the sensibilities of humans to the sufferings of other creatures and whets the
natural human tendency toward savagery and viciousness as hunters do not satisfy
themselves with killing animals harmful to humans but even wipe out tame and
harmless species. In his reference to the escalating cruelty of the Athenian Tyrants,
Plutarch touches upon an idea that is often encountered today in discussion of the
psychology of criminals, namely the notion that mistreatment of animals by young
persons frequently serves as a stepping stone to vicious crimes against human beings
perpetrated by individuals who have become increasingly desensitized to the effects
of their own wanton cruelty.

Pros and *Cons* of Hunting

AUTOBULUS: I am quite afraid, my friends, that the encomium on hunting read yesterday may so excessively stir up our young men who enjoy hunting that they will

88

consider everything else trivial or worthless as they devote themselves totally to this pursuit. I think I myself became caught up in the passion for it all over again, despite my age, and I long, like Euripides' Phaedra, "to call to the hounds and pursue the spotted deer," so thoroughly did the lecture touch me as it set forth its solid and convincing arguments.

SOCLARUS: You speak the truth, dear Autobulus. The fellow who read the encomium seemed to me to stir up the rhetoric after a long period of quiet, delighting the young men and celebrating springtime with them. I was especially delighted with his mention of gladiators, and his view that it is not the least reason to praise hunting that, in addition to drawing to itself most of our delight in battles against other human beings that we have either from birth or education, it provides a pure spectacle of force that the passage from Euripides praises thus:

The strength of man is slight, but
With the subtlety of his wits,
He subdues the fearsome spawn
Of sea and land and hill.

AUTOBULUS: But it is from that source, my dear Soclarus, that they say insensibility to suffering came upon humans and the savagery that has a taste for slaughter and has grown accustomed to feeling no repugnance at the blood and wounds of animals on their hunting expeditions but rather to delighting in the slaughter and killing of animals. What happens next is like what occurred at Athens. The first man killed by the Thirty Tyrants, an informer, was said to have deserved death, as did the second and third. But after that, proceeding little by little, they lay hold of just men, and finally they did not spare even the best citizens. Likewise the first person who killed a bear or a wolf was praised for it, and some cow or pig blamed for tasting the sacred grain set before it was considered to deserve slaughter. Thus, the eating of deer and hare and antelope prepared men for the consumption of sheep and, in some locations, of dogs and horses. "The tame goose and the dove that dwells upon the hearth," as Sophocles says, were cut up and torn asunder, not out of hunger as in the case of weasels and cats, but for pleasure and a tasty treat. Hence the murderous and savage tendencies that are innate in human beings were let loose and rendered immune to pity.

(On the Cleverness of Animals 959B–E)

3. Porphyry

Of all the uses to which animals were put in classical society, none was reckoned so essential to the functioning of the state as the sacrifice of animals in religious contexts. Aristotle (*Politics* 1280b37) identifies such sacrifices as one of the primary functions of the city. While many artistic representations survive of processions and other preparations for animal sacrifices in Greek and Roman ceremonies, very few depictions of the act of sacrifice survive, perhaps because the scene must have been ghastly since victims were dispatched by stabbing or slitting of the throat. Despite the inevitable horror of such scenes, few expressions of sympathy for the sufferings of sacrificial animals are found, which may arise from the fact that almost all meat consumed in Greek society, and much of that consumed in Roman society, was the product of such sacrifice.

In time, Christian apologists denounced the practice of blood sacrifice, again not on grounds of sympathy for the victims but because the sacrifice of Christ was considered to have rendered animal sacrifice unnecessary (see, for example, Hebrews 9: 12–14 on Christ as the new sacrifice). Not all pagan philosophers, however, supported the practice of animal sacrifice, although such a position might bring charges of hostility to the state cult. There is evidence that some earlier Greek philosophical sects, in particular those that were more overtly sympathetic toward animals, found a way around this dilemma by arguing that sacrifice acceptable to the gods did not need to involve blood offerings and that grain offerings were equally welcome. Diogenes Laertius, in his life of Pythagoras (VIII. 20), reports that some held that that the philosopher recommended only inanimate sacrifices, although he notes that some held that he abstained only from sacrificing oxen and rams.

The second book of Porphyry's treatise *On Abstinence from Animal Flesh* deals with the practice of sacrifice. In the second chapter of that book, Porphyry allows that some sacrifice of animals may be acceptable, but he prescribes that the true philosopher, that person who is concerned with his spiritual purity, will abstain from consuming the meat of sacrificial animals if he wishes to imitate god. Porphyry tells the reader (III. 5) that he will borrow the material for a number of the chapters that follow (III. 5–32) from Theophrastus. The specific work in question is usually believed to have been the now-lost work entitled *On Piety*, in which Theophrastus had argued that animal sacrifice was a perversion of earlier custom, in which humans had restricted their offerings to the gods to first fruits. For Theophrastus, and later for Porphyry, this abstinence from animal sacrifice was a matter of justice toward animals, a topic treated by Porphyry at length in the third book of *On Abstinence from Animal Flesh* (see pp. 80–81).

The Gods Do Not Want Blood Sacrifices

In the first place, humans sacrificed animals because, as we have said, a greater necessity had held us. Famines and wars were to blame which compelled us to taste flesh. Now, since crops exist, what necessity is there to carry out a sacrifice required by necessity? Secondly, we should give recompense and thanks for kind services in accord with the value of the benefaction, the greatest to those who have done us the most good and selected from that which is most precious, especially if they have themselves provided it. The crops are the fairest and most precious thing that the gods have accorded us, since by means of them they preserve us and allow us to live in a natural way. Thus we should honor them with these gifts. Truly, we should sacrifice only those things by the sacrifice of which we cause no suffering to anyone, for a sacrifice must be, more than anything else, free of harm to all. If someone should say that god gave us animals no less than crops for our use, one should respond that some harm is caused to them when animals are sacrificed because we deprive them of their souls. They should therefore not be sacrificed. A sacrifice is, according to its name, something holy, and no one is holy if he repays benefactions from the possessions of others without their permission, even if he removes their crops or plants. How can it be holy if those deprived are victims of injustice? If he who takes the crops of others does not sacrifice even those while preserving holiness intact, it is not at all holy for those who take things more valuable than crops to sacrifice them, for the wrong becomes greater thereby. Soul is much more valuable than those things which grow from the ground, and it is not right to take it away through sacrifice.

Therefore we too shall sacrifice, but we will, as is appropriate, offer different sacrifices to different powers. To a god who rules us all, as some wise man has said, we will sacrifice nothing that is perceived by the senses, either by burning or in words. For there is nothing material that is not at once impure to the immaterial. Hence not even language expressed in words is suitable to this god, nor either internal language when it is defiled by the soul's passion. We worship him in pure silence and in pure thoughts about him. We must therefore be joined with him and be made like him, offering the uplifting of our souls as a holy sacrifice to the god, since it is our hymn and our salvation. The sacrifice is carried out in dispassion of the soul and in complete contemplation of the god. We must add the singing of hymns to his offspring, the perceptible gods. The sacrifice is the offering to each god of some of that which he has given to us, from which he sustains us and from which he preserves our existence. As a farmer offers up some of his sheaves and fruits, so shall we offer up our noble thoughts about the gods, rendering thanks for those things that they have given us to contemplate and for the fact that they nourish us truly through the contemplation of themselves, being present to us and appearing to us and shining out for our salvation.

(*On Abstinence from Animal Flesh* II. 12, 34)

Suggestions for Further Reading

1. Plato

Anderson, J.K., *Hunting in the Ancient World* (Berkeley: University of California Press, 1985). This standard work discusses hunting from Homer through the late Roman Empire, concentrating on sport hunting. Organized by historical periods, the work contains a useful index of passages in ancient literature that discuss hunting.

Barringer, Judith M., *The Hunt in Ancient Greece* (Baltimore: Johns Hopkins University Press, 2001). Barringer analyzes what the hunt meant in archaic and classical Greece, and makes much use of evidence from Greek pottery.

Cartmill, Matt, *A View to a Death in the Morning: Hunting and Nature through History* (Cambridge, MA: Harvard University Press, 1993). This fascinating work, thematically organized, discusses man's urge to kill and his shame at killing animals throughout history.

Hughes, J. Donald, "Hunting in the Ancient Mediterranean World," in Linda Kalof, ed., *A Cultural History of Animals in Antiquity* (Oxford: Berg, 2007) 47–70. Hughes discusses hunting in ancient societies from prehistoric times through the classical period, with useful comments on the detrimental effects that hunting had on animal populations in Greece and Rome.

2. Plutarch

Martin, Hubert, "Plutarch's *De Sollertia Animalium* 959B–C: The Discussion of the Encomium on Hunting," *AJPh* 100 (1979) 99–106. Martin analyzes the problems raised by Plutarch's allusion to a treatise on hunting in the opening chapters of *On the Cleverness of Animals*, and concludes that the encomium mentioned is a real work but not a composition of Plutarch.

Tovar Paz, Francisco-Javier, "El Motivo de la 'Caza' in *De Sollertia Animalium* de Plutarco," in José Antonio Fernández and Francisca Pordomingo Pardo, eds, *Estudios sobre Plutarco: Aspectos Formales* 211–217. The author maintains that Plutarch is hostile to hunting and subtly allows his interlocutor Autobulus to suggest that the practice blunts human sensibilities.

3. Porphyry

Obbink, Dirk, "The Origins of Greek Sacrifice: Theophrastus on Religion and Cultural History." The author discusses Theophrastus' lost treatise *On Piety* as the source of the philosopher's views on sacrifices acceptable to the gods, and he tackles the question of Porphyry's debt to that treatise.

6

ANIMALS AS SPORT: THE ARENA

1. Cicero

The use of animals in entertainment can be traced in Greek society to such Bronze Age spectacles as the bull leaping contests depicted on Cretan freezes (*c.*1500 BCE), an activity whose meaning has been variously interpreted but which certainly fascinated spectators as an illustration of the triumph of human strength and wit over the sheer power of wild nature. One is most likely, however, to associate animal entertainments with Roman arena sports, a type of activity that again bore a number of symbolic meanings to spectators. Viewers were reminded of the power of human beings, of the astonishing variety of exotic species that inhabited the vast empire of Rome, and of the violence of savage beasts. Ironically, the systematic slaughter of thousands of rare and beautiful animals suggested to the Romans the superiority of human civilization over the bloodthirsty savagery of wild nature.

Modern scholars have often remarked on the sheer numbers of wild animals dispatched in arena sports, which led to the extinction of some types of mammals and reptiles in certain parts of the empire. In north Africa, for example, the elephant, the rhinoceros and the zebra were wiped out. Suetonius reports (*Titus* 7. 3) that on one day alone, five thousand large animals died in the course of "hunts" and other sports staged in the Colosseum. What is surprising is the fact that the Romans, even professional philosophers among them, seldom felt moved to voice disapproval much less horror at such activities, and the infrequent expressions of disgust that do survive are expressions of dismay at the brutalizing effects of arena sports on human beings, both on those who were forced to participate and on those who chose to watch, rather than of sympathy for the sufferings of the animals.

The incident to which Cicero alludes in the excerpt below from a letter to his friend Marcus Marius is an exception to this rule. In 55 BCE, Pompey offered games to celebrate the opening of his theater at Rome, including a battle with elephants. Pliny the Elder (*Natural History* VIII. 7. 20–21) reports that on this occasion, the elephants fought valiantly against their human tormentors, but when they realized that they were outmatched, they attempted to gain the sympathy of the spectators with their cries and gestures. The audience wept at the sight and rose up in anger against Pompey. Cicero's brief description of this incident, in a letter that consoles Marius for not being able to attend the games, not only mentions the compassion (*misericordia*) that the spectators felt for the animals, but speculates that their reaction was inspired by a belief in a fellowship (*societas*) between humans and other species. This is noteworthy when we recall that Cicero had denied such a fellowship between species in his discussion of the Stoic concept of *oikeiōsis* (see pp. 75–77).

Killing of Arena Animals Arouses Indignation in Spectators

There remain the animal hunts, twice daily over five days, and (no one denies it) magnificent. But what pleasure can there be for a refined person when either a weak human being is ripped apart by an exceedingly powerful beast or a splendid beast is pierced through with a hunting spear? If this sort of thing ought to be witnessed, you have seen it often enough. Nor did I, who was present at it, see anything new in it. The last day was devoted to the elephants. The crowd and mob was quite awed by that, but felt no pleasure. In truth, a kind of compassion actually followed this, and a belief that there exists a sort of fellowship between that type of beast and humankind.

(Epistulae ad familiares [Letters to His Friends] VII. 1. 3)

2. Seneca

The Stoic philosopher Seneca alludes in the passage translated below from his treatise *De brevitate vitae* (*On the Shortness of Life*) to the arena combat with elephants offered by Pompey in 55 BCE which Cicero describes in his letter to Marcus Marius excerpted above, but Seneca's interpretation of the scene differs sharply from that of Cicero, who was himself hardly an advocate for animals in most of his pronouncements. In boldly anthropocentric terms, Seneca laments both the sufferings of human beings subjected to horrific deaths in the arena and the attendant degradation that those who view such spectacles experience. No sympathy is spared for the sufferings of the animals themselves. Seneca reflects not on the cruelty of Pompey in staging such combats but on his arrogance in supposing himself above nature itself in subjecting human beings to such treatment. He ends his comments with the moralizing reflection that in his degrading death on an Egyptian shore at the hands of a minion of King Ptolemy XIII (48 BCE), Pompey showed how undeserved his epithet Magnus ("the Great") had proven.

In his famous condemnation of arena sports (*Epistulae Morales* [*Moral Letters*] 7. 2–4), Seneca again offers no sympathy for the beasts forced to take part in such displays, but his point here is how detrimental bad company can prove for human beings who debase themselves by associating with individuals with corrupted tastes.

Killing of Humans, Not of Animals, in the Arena is Lamentable

Nothing is so detrimental to good character as relaxing at some public show, for then do the vices more readily steal over us through the experience of pleasure. What do you suppose I'm talking about? I come home more covetous, more ambitious, more wanton, in truth more cruel and inhumane, because I have been among human beings. By chance I attended a midday arena show, expecting amusement and good taste and relaxation through which men's eyes gain some rest from human bloodshed. The opposite proved true. The earlier combats were mercy itself by comparison. Now the lighter combats had been put aside and slaughter of men remained. They have nothing with which to protect themselves, and since their whole bodies are exposed to blows, no one strikes in vain. Many prefer this to the usual pairs and the combats by request, and why not? The sword is met with no helmet or shield. What is the point of protection or skill? These just put off death. In the morning the men are thrown to the lions and bears, and in the afternoon to the spectators.

(*Moral Letters* 7. 2–4)

You will perhaps allow men to be interested in the fact that Lucius Sulla was the first to show lions released in the arena, when otherwise they were exhibited chained, and that javelin throwers were sent in by King Bocchus to slay them. This too may be forgiven. But is it of any value to know that Pompey was the first to stage a combat of eighteen elephants in the arena, with criminals sent in to slay them in a battle-scene? He, a leader of the state and a man of outstanding goodness among the foremost figures of previous ages, as his reputation held, thought it a memorable sort of spectacle to kill men in a new manner. Do they fight to the death? That's not enough. Are they torn to bits? That's not enough. Let them be crushed by the enormous bulk of the beasts!

It would be better if such actions should be forgotten lest some powerful figure in future learn of this and envy this action which can hardly be considered the work of a human being. O what darkness does great prosperity cast onto our minds! He believed himself beyond the power of nature when he cast so many troops of human beings beneath beasts born under foreign skies, when he sent into battle such unevenly-matched combatants, when he, who would soon pour forth even more blood himself, spilled such torrents of blood in the sight of the Roman people. But he offered himself up to be pierced through by the lowliest slave when he had been taken in by Alexandrian treachery and he finally realized the empty boast of his epithet, ["the Great"].

(*De brevitate vitae* [*On the Shortness of Life*] 13. 6–7)

Suggestions for Further Reading

Cicero and Seneca

Hughes, J. Donald, *Ecology in Ancient Civilizations* (Albuquerque: University of New Mexico Press, 1975). Hughes discusses the devastating influence that the Roman appetite for arena sports had on the animal populations of Africa and Asia.

Shelton, Jo-Ann, "Beastly Spectacles in the Ancient Mediterranean World," in Linda Kalof, ed., *A Cultural History of Animals in Antiquity* 97–126. Shelton discusses animals in both sacrificial and entertainment contexts from the Greek Bronze Age through Roman imperial times, with emphasis on Roman arena sports.

7

ANIMALS AS FOOD: VEGETARIANISM AND ITS OPPONENTS

1. Diogenes Laertius

Although the mysterious philosopher Pythagoras (6th century BCE) is regularly cited as antiquity's most passionate advocate of the vegetarian lifestyle and is accorded a kind of veneration in the literature of the modern animal rights movement, little is in fact known for certain about the nature, limit and reasons for his support for abstinence, as the passage below from Diogenes Laertius' life of the philosopher makes clear. Since Pythagoras seems to have made some version of the doctrine of metempsychosis, or transmigration of souls, a central feature of his system (see pp. 4–5), it is possible, as Diogenes implies in his mention of the philosopher's belief in the commonality of souls, that Pythagoras opposed the eating of flesh because of the possibility that one might consume a fellow-human whose soul had passed into an animal. In that case, abstinence becomes primarily a matter of spiritual purity, with, as Diogenes notes, the second-ary advantage of improving the mental and spiritual health of the abstinent. One might argue that a vegetarian regimen is in the final analysis self-interested and anthropocentric.

It is noteworthy that Diogenes does not here impute any specifically ethical motivation to Pythagorean abstinence. The idea, frequently attributed to Pythagoras in modern discussions of the philosopher's teachings, that consider-ations of kindness to animals and aversion to the cruelty involved in a meat diet prompted Pythagoras to argue for kindness to animals, receives its most devel-oped expression in a speech attributed to the philosopher in Ovid (*Metamorphoses* XV. 75–142; translated on pp. 99–100). In addition, Plutarch (*On the Cleverness of Animals* 959F) states that "the Pythagoreans" advocated kindness to animals in an effort to instill in humans the desire to treat other humans with kindness, although there too, Pythagoras' motivation might be considered somewhat anthropocen-tric. In the final analysis, Pythagoras' stance on abstinence from animal food remains cloudy, as Diogenes' discussion of Pythagoras' recommendations on the diet of athletes suggests.

Reasons for Pythagoras' Prohibition on the Eating of Meat

[Pythagoras] is said to have been the first to train athletes on a meat diet, starting with Eurymenes, according to what Favorinus says in the third book of his *Memorabilia*, when previous athletes had trained on a diet of dried figs, soft cheese and even wheat, as Favorinus says in the eighth book of his *Miscellaneous History*. Some say a certain trainer named Pythagoras instituted this diet, not the philosopher, since he forbade the killing, not to mention the eating, of animals that have a soul in common with us. This was the ostensible reason, but the actual reason for his prohibition against touching meat was to train and accustom humans to being satisfied with a simple life, so that they could have an easily-obtainable diet, setting before themselves uncooked foods and drinking water, for from that source arise health of body and sharpness of mind.

(*Lives of the Philosophers* VIII. 13 [from the life of Pythagoras])

2. Ovid

What is perhaps the most intriguing exposition of Pythagoras' teaching on abstinence from animal food is found in an unlikely context, namely in a speech attributed to the philosopher in the fifteenth and final book of the *Metamorphoses*, the vast mythological epic by the Roman poet Ovid (43 BCE–17 CE). The long first section of the philosopher's speech, translated below, is an impassioned and sometimes gory plea for the vegetarian lifestyle (XV. 75–142). The longer second half of Pythagoras' speech (XV. 143–478) presents a lengthy account of his views of cosmology, as Ovid interpreted them, and culminates in an explication of his doctrine of transmigration of souls (XV. 459–478). The poetic context of Ovid's portrait of Pythagorean abstinence demands a cautious approach to its ideas, and the passage has been subjected to searching criticism.

In the opening section of *Metamorphoses* XV (1–59), Ovid relates that Numa, the second of Rome's seven legendary kings, met Pythagoras when the king stopped at Croton in the course of an educational tour of Italy, and that the philosopher lectured him on his views. Even in antiquity, the chronological difficulty of such an encounter was noted, since Numa would have lived more than a century before Pythagoras. Ovidian scholars have questioned the very inclusion of the speech at the end of a poem otherwise rather light-hearted in tone, none of whose other characters is a historical personage (Julius Caesar and Augustus are mentioned but do not take part in the narrative action of the poem). Some have dismissed the speech as longwinded, vapid and without significance to the overall structure of the poem. Still others have considered the philosopher's speech a kind of satire on Pythagorean doctrine because of its exaggerated and bombastic rhetoric. At the same time, some scholars have taken Pythagoras' speech as proof that Ovid was himself a vegetarian and that he used the philosopher as the mouthpiece for his own beliefs.

While it would probably be dangerous to draw conclusions on Ovid's food choices on the basis of a section from his epic, a number of conclusions can be drawn from the opening section of Pythagoras' speech translated below. Although the philosopher does touch on the possibility that human souls can take up residence in animals near the conclusion of Pythagoras' exposition (XV. 456–461), the topic is not broached in the opening section of the speech (XV. 75–142). Here, the poet imagines Pythagoras making a somewhat juridical argument for abstention: it is a crime (*scelus*, 88) for human beings to adopt the dietary habits of animals that subsist on each other, although humans may justly (*salva pietate* 109) slay animals that seek the death of humans beings. Ovid seems to hint here at the ancient concept of the "just war" that humans wage against their natural animal enemies, but he denies that humans can justly kill tame and harmless animals that are after all our partners in labor. Ovid's Pythagoras agrees with Theophrastus, in Porphyry's account (see pp. 90–91), that the gods themselves do not seek the death of harmless creatures in sacrifice to them. At least in this earlier part of Pythagoras' speech, Ovid allows the philosopher to argue for abstention on grounds of concern for the sufferings of other living creatures that deserve human kindness, and not on more anthropocentric considerations of personal spiritual purity.

Pythagoras Begs Humans to Spare Animals and Live the Simple Life

[Pythagoras:] "O ye mortals! Refrain from polluting your bodies with accursed foods! There are grain crops, and apples that draw down the branches with their weight, and grapes that grow fat on the vine; there are sweet herbs and those that fire makes delicate and mild, nor do you want for milk or honey or fragrant thyme. The bountiful earth sends up its ripe and rich produce, and provides banquets free of slaughter and gore. Wild beasts still their hunger with blood, and not even all of them: the horse and cattle and flocks of sheep live on grass, but those that have a fierce and untamed nature, Armenian tigers and raging lions and wolves and bears, delight in bloody feasts. O what a crime it is that flesh is swallowed by flesh and that one greedy body grows fat off another body stuffed inside it, and that one living being survives off the death of another! Can it be that, out of such bounty which earth, the best of mothers, provides, you enjoy nothing but chewing at horrid wounds with savage teeth, copying the banquets of the Cyclopes? Can you not assuage the hunger of your greedy stomach that will not rest unless you destroy another creature?

That former age, which we call golden, was rich in the splendid produce of trees that the earth nourishes and did not pollute its mouth with gore. Then birds were safe to move about the trees, and the hare wandered carefree in the middle of the fields, nor had the trusting nature of fishes caused them to hang from a hook. Everything was free of deceit, heedless of trickery, and full of peace. Later some noxious individual, whoever it was, envied the food of the gods and buried flesh in his greedy belly: he prepared the way for crime. It may be that at first the knife grew warm when stained with the blood of wild beasts (that was enough!), and we admit that those creatures that sought our death were justly sent to their death. But those beasts that were rightly killed should not be devoured!

After that, crime reached further, and first the pig was believed to have deserved to die, a victim because it rooted up seed with its curving snout and stole the hope of the year's crops. The goat was slaughtered at the altar of vengeful Bacchus for eating his vines. These two creatures died because of their own crimes. But how did sheep deserve this, a gentle flock born to dwell among humans, bearing their nectar in full udders, creatures that provide us their wool for clothing and delight us more in their lives than in their deaths? How did oxen deserve this, creatures free of deceit and treachery, innocent and pure, born for labor? He is unmindful of this and unworthy of the fruits of the earth who, having removed the weight of the curved plow from its neck, could kill his helpmate at the tiller, striking with his ax the neck that so often renewed the intractable field and gave him so many harvests.

It was not enough that such a crime is committed: they involved the gods themselves in their crime and maintain that the gods above delight in the slaughter of the hard-working bullock. He stands, a victim without blemish and splendid in form (that is what caused his downfall!), decked out with fillets and gold before the altar, and hears without comprehending the priest's prayer and sees placed on his forehead, between his horns, the grain that his own labor produced, and, when struck, he dyes with blood the knife that he perhaps sees coated with his own gore. At once they inspect the entrails snatched from his still-heaving breast and dig about in them to learn the will of the gods. You dare to eat of that, ye mortal men? Is man's hunger for forbidden food so great? I beg you, forebear to do that and heed my warning. When you place the limbs of that slain creature in your mouth, take thought of the fact that you chew upon your own field-mate."

(*Metamorphoses* XV. 75–142)

3. Empedocles

In his life of the Presocratic philosopher Empedocles (*c*.492–432 BCE), Diogenes Laertius states (VIII. 77) that he composed two philosophical poems entitled *Peri phuseōs* (*On Nature*) and *Katharmoi* (*Purifications*), totaling five thousand verses. Some scholars believe the two titles refer in fact to the same work, and even among those who consider them to be distinct poems, there is no agreement as to which fragments should be attributed to which work. The most famous Empedoclean doctrine is that the cosmos consists of four elements – air, earth, fire and water – which come together and separate under the influence of forces which the philosopher calls *philia* ("friendship," "attraction") and *neikos* ("strife," "repulsion"). It would seem reasonable to conclude that the Empedoclean fragments relating to this cosmological scheme can be attributed to the poem *On Nature*.

The extant fragments of Empedocles indicate that he had much of interest to say on human–animals relations as well, although the fragmentary state of his works at times makes interpretation difficult. Issues of sacrifice, human purity and the kinship of humans and other species are raised, and we may be justified in concluding that these fragments are attributable to *Purifications*. Empedocles expounded a version of the theory of metempsychosis, according to which human and animal souls could inhabit either human or animal bodies in subsequent incarnations. Diogenes Laertius quotes two verses in which Empedocles claims to have been a boy, a maiden, a bush and a fish in various lives. His belief in reincarnation must have contributed significantly to his advocacy of the vegetarian lifestyle. Diogenes reports further (VIII. 53) that Empedocles on one occasion fed some envoys a sacrificial animal fashioned from honey and barley meal. Moreover, Aristotle (*Rhetoric* 1373b14–16) states that Empedocles declared that no human being could justly kill another living being, suggesting that Empedocles believed that a relationship of justice exists between species.

In the longer of the two passages translated below, which appears to contain a break that renders the sequence of thought slightly incoherent, Empedocles admits to having slain other living creatures, which led him into a long period of exile from god during which he was forced to undergo a series of reincarnations, while the shorter fragment, in which he laments having eaten meat, is notable for its suggestion that a human who tears an animal apart for food is himself a beast armed with claws.

What Led Men to Touch Their Lips to Gore?

There is an oracle of necessity, an ancient decree of the gods, everlasting, sealed with broad oaths: whenever someone stains his own limbs with slaughter in his misguidedness ... will swear falsely after committing a misdeed, the gods who have been granted long-lasting life, he wanders three times ten thousand seasons away from the blessed ones, passing into all shapes of mortal things over time, exchanging the painful paths of life. For the powers of the air pursue him into the sea, and the sea spits him onto the plain of earth, and earth into the rays of burning sun, and the sun casts him into the eddies of air. One after another receives him, but all hate him. I too am one of these now, in exile from god and a wanderer, trusting in raging strife.

Alas! If only the pitiless day had destroyed me before I devised horrible deeds with my claws for the sake of food!

(Fragments 11 and 124 Inwood [= "Empedocles," DK 115 and 139])

4. Plato

A number of factors have led some scholars to conclude that Plato pursued a vegetarian regimen in his own life and recommended it for others. Some evidence for this survives in anecdotes contained in ancient biographies of the philosopher. Diogenes Laertius, for example, records in his life of the Cynic Diogenes (VI. 25–26) that Plato admitted to having lived mainly on olives while visiting Sicily, and he reports that Plato was known to have been quite fond of figs. A more substantial piece of evidence, though still circumstantial, is Plato's attraction to Pythagorean teachings. Cicero relates (*Tusculan Disputations* I. 39) that Plato visited Italy in order to study Pythagoreanism in detail and that he adopted the older thinker's teachings enthusiastically. The doctrine of metempsychosis, in one or another of its manifestations, appears in a number Plato's dialogues (see pp. 4–5). Despite such apparent evidence for Plato's support for abstention, and references in ancient literature to Plato's generally austere lifestyle, it would be dangerous to draw firm conclusions on the philosopher's own dietary practices from such evidence. As was noted above, Plato, in a discussion of hunting (*Laws* 824b), condemns fishing while recommending hunting with dogs and horses as a pursuit worthy of a free man.

It is with such considerations in mind that the excerpts below from the *Republic* and the *Laws* must be viewed. In *Republic* 372a–d, Socrates, in a passage sometimes taken as evidence that he was himself a vegetarian, envisions a lifestyle in the ideal state that would be supported by the simplest of foods, specifically vegetarian fare, which is declared to promote good health and long life. Since this idyllic picture is a vision of the ideal state, it is difficult to determine whether Plato, or his mouthpiece Socrates, believed it achievable, and it may be that Plato's interest here lies more in the creation of a society whose austere lifestyle would make it more inclined to seek philosophical enlightenment while avoiding luxurious distractions, than in the particulars of diet. Some scholars have suspected that the portrait of parents and children singing hymns the gods while sitting on straw and sporting garlands may be slightly comical in intent.

In the same way that Plato envisions a vegetarian regimen for his ideal state, so does he suppose that early man lived on a diet that nature provided freely and generously and that eliminated the necessity for humans to harm other species either for food or in sacrifice. Classical accounts of the early days of man often assumed that our ancestors lived on friendly terms with other species and fed predominantly, although not perhaps exclusively, on fruits and grains. Some accounts of such a "Golden Age" existence (for example, Hesiod, *Works and Days* 109–126 and Ovid, *Metamorphoses* I. 89–112) strongly imply, but do not explicitly state, that early humans pursued a vegetarian lifestyle. In the passage below from *Laws*, Plato does claim that early man abstained from meat, in a passage that suggests Pythagorean influence in its mention of the "Orphic life," since followers of the legendary singer Orpheus supposedly believed, as did the Pythagoreans, in metempsychosis and consequently practiced abstention.

Diet in the Ideal State

[SOCRATES:] "First of all, let us consider what sort of life they will lead who are thus provided for. Will they not make food and wine and clothing and shoes? And they will construct houses and in summer work unclothed and barefoot, and in winter clothed and adequately shod. And too they will produce meal from barley and flour from wheat. Some of this they will cook and some knead, offering up excellent cakes and bread on some sort of reeds or clean leaves. Reclining on straw beds strewn with yew and myrtle, they and their children will feast together, drinking wine, while crowned with garlands and singing hymns to the gods, enjoying each other's company, begetting no more offspring than they can afford and having a care for poverty and war."

Here Glaucon interrupted, "Your men, it appears, dine without relishes?"

"You are right," I said, "I had forgotten that they will have relishes: salt, obviously, and olives and cheese, and onions and greens of the sort that they boil in the country. For dessert we will provide them some figs and chickpeas and beans. They will roast myrtle-berries and acorns at the fire while drinking in moderation. Living thus in peace and health, they will die in old age, it seems likely, and will hand on such a life to their children."

(Republic 372a–d)

The Diet of Early Man

ATHENIAN: "Let us go back then to what we said initially. Each person should reflect on this: the human race either had no beginning and will have no end, but existed and always shall, or it has been an incomprehensible period of time since it came into existence."

KLEINIAS: "Of course."

ATHENIAN: "Well, do we not then suppose that cities have risen and fallen, and that all sorts of institutions of order and disorder have appeared, and that all kinds of appetites for food, both drinks and meats, existed over the entire earth, and every change of seasons, in which it is likely animals underwent numerous transformations?"

KLEINIAS: "Surely."

ATHENIAN: "And do we believe that vines that had not previously existed appeared at some point? Did the olive and the gifts of Demeter and Persephone appear then? And was some Triptolemus minister of such products? And do we not suppose that at that time, when these foods did not exist, animals fed on one another as they do now?"

KLEINIAS: "Certainly."

ATHENIAN: "We see that the practice of humans sacrificing each other continues even today in many peoples. On the other hand, we hear that among other peoples no one dared to taste of an ox, and that they sacrificed not animals but meal and cakes steeped in honey, and other such innocent offerings. And they kept away from flesh as being unholy to consume and they refrained from polluting altars of the gods with blood. Those of us who existed then lived the so-called 'Orphic life,' allowing all inanimate foods but at the same time keeping clear of all animate foods."

KLEINIAS: "What you say is much reported and easily believable."

ATHENIAN: "'Why,' someone might ask, 'was all of this told to us?'"

KLEINIAS: "A correct supposition, stranger."

ATHENIAN: "If I can, I shall attempt to explain what topic comes next in order."

KLEINIAS: "Please go on."

ATNENIAN: "I see that all things among human beings depend upon three sorts of needs and desires. If humans conduct themselves correctly with regard to these, goodness results, but if badly, the opposite occurs. Among these, the desire for food and drink arises at birth, and every living creature has a desire for this aspect of life in its entirety and is full of passion for it, being unwilling to heed anyone who suggests that he do anything but satisfy his desires and cravings for these in every respect, and thereby remove all pain. The third and greatest need and desire, which, though arising last, is most acute, leaves humans on fire with mad passion: that which inflames humans with the intense desire to beget offspring. We must attempt to direct these three desires toward the good rather than toward that which is apparently the most pleasant, and to check them with those three principles which are greatest: fear, law and true reason, availing ourselves of the Muses and the gods of the games to extinguish their growth and flow."

(*Laws* 781e–783b)

5. Seneca

The Stoic Seneca's account of his short-lived flirtation with the vegetarian lifestyle (*Epistulae Morales* [*Moral Letters*] 108) is fascinating on several grounds. In the brief compass of this letter, Seneca has occasion to mention virtually every sort of argument put forward in antiquity to justify abstention, and some that appear in modern discussions as well, and it is striking how sympathetically and passionately Seneca presents arguments that he would later, as a Stoic, reject. In the sections of the letter preceding the excerpt translated below, Seneca tells his correspondent Lucilius that he had been persuaded by the Stoic Attalus, one of his early teachers, to shun pleasures and luxuries, advice that he never ignored (*Moral Letters* 108. 13–16). Even in old age, he reports, he avoided oysters and mushrooms as foods that stir the appetite and hinder digestion (108. 15).

The topic of simple living leads Seneca to elaborate his account of his early philosophical education and to take up the subject of his experimentation with vegetarianism. His teacher Sotion, a Peripatetic from Alexandria, practiced abstention primarily on Pythagorean grounds, believing that a human ran the risk of devouring a family member whose soul had passed into the body of an animal, but he taught Seneca that Sextius, a Greek philosopher with Stoic leanings but Pythagorean sympathies who had a loyal following for a time at Rome (early 1st century CE), emphasized considerations of kindness to animals and good human hygiene in his defense of vegetarianism, arguments common in modern literature on the benefits of a vegetarian regime but less frequently encountered in ancient discussions of the topic. Similarly, Seneca admits to improved mental function while following a meatless diet, another advantage frequently cited in modern vegetarian literature. The ease with which he ultimately abandoned his practice of abstention, a change which he characterizes as the inauguration of better mealtimes (*inciperem melius cenare*, 108. 22), suggests the shallowness of his original commitment, and although Seneca practiced an austere lifestyle into old age, there is no evidence that he ever adopted the vegetarianism lifestyle again.

The Philosopher Took Up Vegetarianism but Soon Abandoned It

Since I have begun to explain to you how I came to philosophy with greater enthusiasm as a young man than I pursue it as an old one, I shall not be ashamed to confess to you what passion Pythagoras inspired in me. Sotion used to explain why he and later Sextius abstained from animal food. Each had a different reason, but each reason was splendid. The latter of these believed that man had enough food without resorting to bloodshed, and that a habit of cruelty was born when this tearing of flesh became a matter of pleasure. He added too that the opportunity for extravagance ought to be reduced, in the belief that a varied diet is contrary to good nutrition and foreign to our bodies. But Pythagoras said that there was a kinship among all creatures and that there exists an exchange of souls that pass into other forms. If you believe him, no soul perishes, and does not even cease to be except for a very short time during which it is being passed into another body. We shall investigate later through what periods of time and after how many exchanges of residence the soul returns to a human being. For the moment, we note that he inspired in humans a fear of crime and of parricide since persons could unknowingly come upon the soul of a parent and profane it with knife and tooth, if the spirit of some relative might be dwelling in the body consumed.

After Sotion had set forth this argument and supplemented it with his own, he said, "Do you not believe that souls are distributed to one body after another and that what we call death is actually a migration? Do you not believe that what was once a human being's soul dwells in these cattle or wild beasts or sea creatures? Do you not believe that nothing perishes in this world but rather changes place, or that celestial bodies are not alone in passing through definite circuits, but that animals too move in cycles and are propelled through a celestial course? Great men have believed these things. Therefore withhold judgment, remain open to the entire topic. If this position is true, abstention from animal flesh constitutes blamelessness; if it is false, it constitutes frugality. What loss is there in your believing it? I am depriving you of the food of lions and vultures!"

I was inspired by these teachings to become a vegetarian, and the habit proved not only easy but pleasant after one year's practice. I believed my mind was more acute, though today I would not swear to you that it was. You ask how I gave up the practice? My early manhood took place during the first part of the reign of Tiberius. At that time foreign cults were making the rounds, and abstention from meat was advanced as proof of adherence to certain cults. On the urging of my father, who did not so much fear false accusation as he hated philosophy, I returned to my former habits, and he had no difficulty in persuading me to have a better diet.

(Moral Letters **108. 17–23)**

6. Plutarch

Plutarch is the earliest classical author from whom there survives a work devoted entirely to the defense of the vegetarian lifestyle. His treatise *De esu carnium* (*On the Eating of Flesh*), in two parts that seem to belong together and that exhibit some gaps and instances of interpolation from other works of uncertain authorship, is, despite these issues of transmission, invaluable for the insights it provides us into the breadth and variety of arguments that were marshaled in antiquity in defense of abstention. Not the least interest that the treatise holds for us is its surprisingly "modern" tone, since Plutarch builds a case for abstention that employs a number of arguments commonly encountered in the literature of the modern animal rights movement while underplaying other arguments that one might have expected to encounter prominently in an ancient defense of vegetarianism.

As is the case with all ancient writers who portray a vegetarian regimen in a sympathetic light, scholars have debated whether we are justified in concluding that Plutarch himself was an adherent to that lifestyle. Some have maintained that a certain immature tone to the treatise *On the Eating of Flesh* suggests that Plutarch had indeed been a vegetarian in his younger years but abandoned the practice when he had developed a more sensible attitude toward life. We can say with certainty only that Plutarch does not present a completely consistent position on abstention, since the first excerpt below, from his treatise on maintaining good health, suggests that he at least conceded that the widespread practice of meat eating, however lamentable, must be accepted but kept to a minimum because of the detrimental effects of meat to human health and mental acuity.

The heated rhetoric that some scholars have detected in Plutarch's pronounce-ments on the evils of meat eating are evident in the excerpts from *On the Eating of Flesh* included below, some of which will be strikingly recognizable to readers famil-iar with the literature of the modern vegetarian movement. The idea that human beings took up meat rather out of a desire for variety in diet than from necessity, since the earth produces plenty of nutritious and wholesome foods that would easily sustain humans without the need to resort to cruelty, appears in various guises in contemporary vegetarian polemic, and Plutarch's suggestion (*On the Eating of Flesh* 995E) that the eating of meat is "contrary to nature" (*para phusin*) may hint at the argument, common in defenses of the vegetarian lifestyle today, that the human being is anatomically unsuited to the consumption of meat. He makes this argu-ment specifically at *On the Eating of Flesh* 994F, where he declares the human being "not carnivorous by nature," and at 995D, translated below.

It is worth noting that Plutarch relies very little, in developing his case for absten-tion from meat, on Pythagorean considerations of transmigration of souls. In fact, in the opening sentence of *On the Eating of Flesh* (993A), he states that he would rather investigate why humans ever took up the consumption of meat than inquire into Pythagoras' reasons for opposing the practice. He does at least allow (*On the Eating of Flesh* 998D) that, although no one has ever proven the concept of transmigration of souls, the possibility might give us pause in contemplating our dietary choices.

Unparalleled in ancient literature and strikingly modern is Plutarch's portrait (*On the Eating of Flesh* 996E–997A) of the horrors endured by animals being raised and slaughtered for human consumption, details of which recall exposés of the gruesome practices of modern factory farms where animals intended for human use endure short and miserable lives, fed hormones to increase their size and improve the taste of their flesh and often spending their lives entirely in darkness before being beaten and kicked on their way to slaughter.

Meat Eating Has Become a Perverse Second Nature among Humans

It is best to accustom the body not to need meat in addition to its other foods, for the earth offers its bounteous products not only for our nourishment but also for our enjoy-ment and comfort, providing some gifts for our use with no added effort and others that may be enjoyed in all sorts of combinations. But since custom has become a sort of "second nature contrary to nature," we should not use the consumption of meat for the satisfaction of our hunger, in the manner of wolves or lions, but merely adding meat to our foods as a sort of support and undergirding to our diet. We should use other foods and edibles which are most in accord with the nature of our bodies and have less of a dulling effect on our reason which is, so to speak, kindled by plain and light-weight material.

(*De sanitate tuenda praecepta* [*Precepts for Preserving Health*] 131F–132A)

Meat is Unnecessary to Humans

Everyone might maintain that the reason those first men took up the eating of flesh was their need and difficult circumstances. It was not while they were living in the midst of unlawful desires and in an abundance of necessities that they turned to such a practice, after luxuriating in unnatural and exotic pleasures. If they took on sensation and voice at this moment, they would declare, "O you beloved of the gods, you who live in the present day, what an age have you been granted that you enjoy and harvest a boundless lot of good things! What plants grow for you, what vineyards! What wealth from the earth, what delights from trees are here for the picking! You can live in luxury without slaughter. We were welcomed into the more miserable and frightening epoch of the world, we who fell at our birth into the greatest and most intractable poverty. The atmosphere concealed the heaven and the stars while befouled with thick and unstable moisture and fire and windstorms. 'Not yet was the sun set in his course:

Keeping his path, dividing dawn and dusk,
He led them back again, and crowned them
With the fruitful, flower-garlanded hours,
And earth was outraged'

by the lawlessness, as streams of rivers and most parts were made misshapen marshes and laid waste by muddy depths and sterile thickets and woods. Cultivated plants did not yet exist, nor tools nor any instrument of skill. Our hunger gave us no rest, and no seed awaited the annual planting season.

What wonder is it then if we availed ourselves of animal flesh, contrary to nature, when mud itself was eaten and tree bark was devoured, and it was a matter of good fortune to come upon sprouting grass or a piece of reed? We danced from joy around the oak-tree when we had tasted and eaten acorns, calling the tree 'life-giving' and 'mother' and 'nursemaid.' That was the sort of celebration our life knew then, while all else was full of wildness and gloom. But what madness and frenzy drive you who live now to blood-thirstiness, you who have such an abundance of necessities? Why do you slander earth by calling her incapable of nourishing you? Why do you dishonor lawgiving Demeter and shame the gentle Dionysus, as if you did not receive sufficient bounty from them? Are you not ashamed to mingle the fruits of the earth with blood and slaughter? You call serpents and panthers and lions savage, when you leave them no room to surpass you in bloodthirstiness. For them, slaughter is the source of their livelihood, but for you it provides a delicacy."

(*On the Eating of Flesh* 993C–994B)

Meat Weighs Down the Human Soul

Now, eating meat is not only contrary to the nature of the human body, but it also weighs down souls through fullness and surfeit. "For wine and generous amounts of meat make the body strong and mighty, but the soul weak." So as not to arouse the hatred of athletes, I'll use my country-folk as examples. The Athenians called the Boeotians dense and dull-witted and stupid, especially because of their gluttony. "For they are swine …," and as Menander says, "They have jaws," and Pindar remarks, "And to learn …," and according to Heraclitus, "The dry soul is wisest." Empty jars resound when struck, but they do not give off sound when full. Delicate bronze objects pass on sound in a circle until you block off and deaden the sound by hindering it as the beat is carried around. The eye when filled with excessive moisture is blurred and rendered weak in fulfilling its proper task. When we see the sun through damp air and coarse exhalations, we do not perceive it as pure and bright but rather as submerged and dimmed and faint in its rays. So too it is absolutely necessary that, when the body is fouled and burdened and overfilled with inappropriate foods, the splendor and brilliance of the soul take on a dullness and confusion, wandering about and going astray, since it does not possess the splendor and force to attain to the fine and subtle tasks of human life.

(*On the Eating of Flesh* 995D–996A)

The Slaughter of Food Animals Is Cruel

If it is in fact impossible to be free of error because of our intimacy with it, we shall be ashamed of our erroneous behavior and shall handle it rationally, eating meat not from wanton luxury but from hunger. We shall kill the animal, but in pity and mental anguish, not treating it harshly or torturing it. This is how many do now who thrust red-hot spits into the throats of swine so that the blood may be refined by the insertion of the iron and may make the meat tender and soft by flowing around it. Others leap upon the udders of sows that are near birthing and kick them, so that, what they have mingled blood and milk and the fetuses have been destroyed, they may (O god!) devour the most inflamed part of the animal. Others sew up the eyes of cranes and swans and shut them away and fatten them up in darkness, making their flesh a dainty treat by mingling it with exotic flavorings and spices.

(*On the Eating of Flesh* 996E–997A)

7. Porphyry

The first book of Porphyry's lengthy defense of vegetarianism, *De abstinentia* (*On Abstinence from Animal Flesh*), provides a valuable survey of *anti*-vegetarian arguments voiced in classical antiquity, each of which is refuted at greater or lesser length in the subsequent books of the treatise. These arguments range from "man in the street" objections (we will be overrun with animals if we do not eat them; we will starve if we allow animals to eat our food; we have always eaten meat) to the more sophisticated arguments of established philosophical schools. Porphyry directs his polemic most vehemently against the Stoics whose doctrine of animal irrationality (see pp. 10–19) released man from any obligation toward other species and by implication condoned the eating of meat. The first passage below introduces the theme of man's kinship with animals when Porphyry states that his opponents (that is, the Stoics) consider justice to be overturned if we believe that animals live in a manner akin (*oikeiōs*, I. 4. 2) to that of human beings. Porphyry developed an extensive case for man's debt of justice toward other species that depended upon a demonstration that other species are indeed rational and therefore do fall under the purview of human justice, fulfilling the Stoic prerequisite for entrance into the moral community. The final sentence of the first excerpt below gives an interesting insight into Porphyry's manner of composition in *On Abstinence from Animal Flesh*, being a verbatim quotation from Plutarch's treatise *On the Cleverness of Animals* (964A). *On Abstinence from Animal Flesh* III. 20–24 consists in a similar manner of almost verbatim citation of *On the Cleverness of Animals* 959E–963F.

Although the second excerpt below is concerned primarily with the central theme of Porphyry's second book, that the gods scorn animal sacrifices and desire offerings that do not entail violence to other animal species, the opening sentences of the passage offer an interesting instance of a slide argument still encountered in modern anti-vegetarian philosophy: if humans refrain from eating animals, perhaps they must likewise refrain from eating plants and non-lethal animal derivatives such as eggs, honey and dairy foods. If animals are spared because they are in some degree sentient, perhaps plants are equally so and consuming them would cause them the same pain and fear that food animals experience at slaughter. Porphyry's refutations of such arguments seem to be derived from the treatise *On Piety* by Theophrastus, whom Porphyry mentions by name as a source for his present discussion (II. 7). He offers several considerations, although he does not specifically address the issue of sentience in plants: plants offer their produce to us on their own and do not die in the process, while we are entitled to harvest both honey and grain crops because human beings look after bees and cultivated fields.

Carnivores Say Meat Eating is Permissible because Animals Are Irrational

Now, our opponents say that justice is immediately thrown into chaos and the immovable moved, if we extend justice not only to the rational but also to the irrational, reckoning not only human beings and the gods to be our kin but including likewise as kin the wild beasts that are in no way related to us, and refraining from using some of them for work and others of them for food, while considering them as different from us in their nature and as having no rights just as they have no common citizenship with us. For he who uses them as one would use human beings, sparing them and not harming them and saddling justice with a burden that it cannot bear, destroys what justice can do and corrupts kinship with that which is foreign to it. Either injustice becomes necessary for us if we do not spare them, or life becomes impossible and unimaginable if we do not use them, and we shall live a kind of beastly life by rejecting the use of beasts.

(On Abstinence from Animal Flesh I. 4)

Plants Are Non-sentient and Therefore Permissible as Food

Perhaps someone might say that we may take something from plants as well, is that not so? But the taking is not the same [as from animals], for it is from beings that are not unwilling. Even if we leave them alone, they drop their fruit and our taking of that fruit is not accompanied by the death of the plants, as happens when animals lose their lives. It is right that the profit should be shared from the harvest of the produce of bees, since that comes from our labors, for the bees gather the honey from the plants and we care for the bees. It is seemly that it be shared in such a way that no harm comes to them: what they do not use but what could be of use to us should be payment from them. We should avoid animals in sacrifice, for everything belongs to the gods but the crops are reckoned to be ours since we sow them and plant them and tend them with other sorts of care. We should sacrifice what is ours, not what belongs to others, since that which is cheap and easily obtained is holier and dearer to the gods than that which is not easily obtained, and that which is most readily available to the sacrificers provides immediate and ceaseless reverence. Therefore, something which is neither holy nor inexpensive, even If at hand, should not be sacrificed at all.

(On Abstinence from Animal Flesh II. 13)

Suggestions for Further Reading

1. Pythagoras (in Diogenes Laertius)

Haussleiter, *Der Vegetarismus in der Antike* 97–157. The author offers an extensive discussion of Pythagoras and his school, with emphasis on the doctrine of metempsychosis as a reason for Pythagoras' case for abstention.

Dombrowski, *The Philosophy of Vegetarianism* 35–54.

Tsekourakis, Damianos, "Pythagoreanism or Platonism and Ancient Medicine? The Reasons for Vegetarianism in Plutarch's 'Moralia'," *ANRW* II. 36, 1 (1987) 366–393. In the third section of this study, Tsekourakis provides a carefully argued analysis of potential reasons for Pythagoras' abstention, concluding that religious and mystical considerations predominated over rational and scientific notions.

2. Pythagoras (in Ovid)

Newmyer, Stephen T., "Ovid on the Moral Grounds for Vegetarianism," in Werner Schubert, ed., *Ovid: Werk und Wirkung: Festgabe für Michael von Albrecht zum 65. Geburtstag*, I (Frankfurt: Peter Lang, 1998) 477–486. This analysis of *Metamorphoses* XV. 60–478 stresses the degree to which Ovid attributes a concern for animal suffering and a belief in human–animal kinship to Pythagoras.

3. Empedocles

Haussleiter 157–163.

Rundin, John, "The Vegetarianism of Empedocles in Its Historical Context," *The Ancient World* 29 (1998) 19–35. Rundin argues that Empedocles' support for abstention may in fact be a political statement in support of democratic ideals directed against Sicilian aristocrats who received the first and largest portions of sacrificed animals.

4. Plato

Haussleiter 184–198. The author emphasizes the difficulty involved in attempting to assess Plato's own position on abstention from his sometimes contradictory pronouncements.

5. Seneca

Haussleiter 257–262. Haussleiter demonstrates how Seneca's apparently positive statements on abstention arose primarily from his opposition to luxuries in human life rather than from any sympathy for animals.

6. Plutarch

Jufresa, Montserrat, "La Abstinencia de Carne y el Origen de la Civilización in Plutarco," in Fernández Delgado and Pardo, eds., *Estudios sobre Plutarco: Aspectos Formales.* The author shows how ethical and scientific considerations are more important to Plutarch's defense of vegetarianism than are any religious ideas.

Newmyer, Stephen T., *Animals, Rights and Reason in Plutarch and Modern Ethics.* Chapter 6, "Animal Appetites," provides a detailed analysis of Plutarch's case for abstention with emphasis on its innovative character and its anticipation of a number of modern arguments for abstention.

——, "Plutarch on the Moral Grounds for Vegetarianism," *CO* 72 (1995) 41–43. This article demonstrates how Plutarch's case for abstention anticipates some defenses of abstention encountered in modern animal rights literature.

7. Porphyry

Dombrowski, Daniel A., "Vegetarianism and the Argument from Marginal Cases in Porphyry," *JHI* 45 (1984) 141–143. Dombrowski shows that Porphyry anticipates the modern ethical stance called the Argument from Marginal Cases at *On Abstinence from Animal Flesh* III. 19, where he argues that since some humans live at the level of sensation alone, we must respect the interests of animals that may be likewise sentient to such a degree. If humans defend the interests of such humans, they cannot justly deny such protection to animals that may function at an equal level.

Haussleiter 316–337. The author's discussion centers primarily on Porphyry's spiritual arguments for abstention that arise from his belief in the doctrine of metempsychosis.

8

ANIMALS AS FRIENDS: KINDNESS TO ANIMALS

1. Homer

Although Greco-Roman literature contains discussions of virtually every conceivable human–animal interaction, descriptions of deliberate and wanton cruelty toward domesticated animals, be they companion animals or farm animals, are almost unexampled, and, as the excerpts below suggest, expressions of disapproval of such treatment did not inevitably arise from sympathy for the sufferings of the mistreated creatures

Homer's descriptions of animals occur most frequently in the context of sometimes extended similes (see p. 40), but his famous account of the neglect and mistreatment of Odysseus' faithful dog Argus during his master's absence at Troy (*Iliad* XVII. 290–323) transcends the stereotypic language and ideas of similes and constitutes the sole example of intentional cruelty to animals in Homer's epics. While it would be dangerous to overinterpret the significance of this passage in the history of classical speculation on interspecies relations, the degree of sympathy between the abused animal that recognizes its master's voice after twenty years' separation and the master who turns away in tears at the sight of his dog, is noteworthy, and the pathos of the scene is intensified when Argus dies shortly after, having seen his beloved master once more (XVII. 326–327).

The Mistreatment of Odysseus' Dog, Argus

So they spoke to one another, and a dog raised his head and pricked up his ears, Argus, the dog of stout-hearted Odysseus who had cared for him once but had had no enjoyment of him before he went off to Troy. The young men had earlier taken him out to hunt goats and deer and hare. But in his master's absence, he lay despised, in a heap of dung by the door which was piled there until Odysseus' servants could take it out to spread on the great estate. Argus lay there, infested with fleas, but when he sensed that Odysseus was near, he wagged his tail and flattened his ears, but he could not move nearer to his master. Seeing this, [Odysseus] wiped away a tear, not letting Eumaius observe this, and said to him, "Eumaius, this dog on the dung-heap is an amazing sight. He is a fine-looking creature, but I cannot say, just looking at him, whether he was swift on the run, or was a lapdog, like those that masters keep for show."

The swineherd Eumaius replied, "This dog belonged to a man who died far away. If he could appear in form and deed as when his master Odysseus left him, you would behold his speed and strength. He would not flee from any wild beast in the depths of the forest nor show it any fear, and he outdid others in tracking. But now he suffers and his master died far from home. The unfeeling women take no care of him. When their masters are no longer in charge of them, they no longer want to work as is proper, for farseeing Zeus takes away half of a man's merit when the day of servitude comes upon him."

(Odyssey **XVII. 290–323)**

2. Diogenes Laertius (a) and Plutarch (b) on Pythagoras

The two accounts below of Pythagoras' objections to cruelty to animals, from Diogenes Laertius' life of the philosopher and from Plutarch's treatise *On the Cleverness of Animals*, suggest motives that arise not solely from the operation of a kindly and humane disposition. When Pythagoras enjoins his companion to refrain from striking a dog, it is because he senses that the soul of a human friend of his has passed into the animal, in keeping with his doctrine of metempsychosis. Similarly, Plutarch's account of the origin of Pythagoras' objection to animal cruelty suggests an indirect duty view on the part of the early philosopher, according to which humans are enjoined to refrain from cruelty to animals because kindness to them promotes kindness to human beings, rather than because such cruelty is *per se* objectionable.

a. Diogenes Laertius: Pythagoras Forbade Kicking of an Animal That He Recognized as a Friend

Xenophanes bore witness to [Pythagoras'] having been one person at one time and another at another time, writing [of him] in his elegies:

"I follow now another way of thought,
And show another path."
This is what he says of him:
"When they passed by a pup that was abused,
He pitied it and said, 'Stop! Strike him not!
He is the soul of my old friend: I knew
Him once I heard his yelp!"

(*Lives of the Philosophers* VIII. 36 [from the life of Pythagoras])

b. Plutarch: Pythagoras Enjoined Kindness to Animals to Promote Kindness to Humans

The Pythagoreans, in contrast, made a practice of kindness toward animals in order to promote love toward human beings and compassion for them, for familiarity has a remarkable ability to advance human beings by working little by little on their innate feelings.

(*On the Cleverness of Animals* 959F)

3. Plutarch

Although animals figure prominently in the collection of Plutarch's ethical treatises known as the *Moralia* (see pp. 15–17), they scarcely appear in his more famous *Parallel Lives* which trace the careers of prominent Greek and Roman political figures. Plutarch makes little effort to account for all the details of his subjects' lives and he seldom provides dates, since his principal interest is in the moral lessons that may be garnered from the actions of his subjects. In the passage below from his life of the Roman politician and writer Marcus Porcius Cato "the Censor" (234–149 BCE), Plutarch endeavors to show the churlish and mean-spirited side of the much-admired Roman by delineating his callous attitude toward slaves and animals that have outlived their productive years. Plutarch's critique of Cato's outlook contains a view of the nature of man's obligation toward animals that is strikingly at odds with his position in the treatises of his *Moralia* since in the life of Cato, Plutarch denies that humans have a debt of justice toward animals which he here calls "irrational" (*aloga*), in contrast to his position in *On the Cleverness of Animals*, but he does assert here that man may at least demonstrate "goodwill" (*euergesias*) and "kindness" (*charitas*) toward them. Although he denies the possibility of a relationship of justice between species, he nevertheless insists that some obligation to treat animals with humane consideration is incumbent upon humans that arises from mankind's good nature.

We Owe Animals at Least Benevolence if Not Justice

[Cato] never bought a slave for more than fifteen hundred drachmas, not needing effeminate or attractive ones but rather hard-working hearty ones for tending horses and oxen. He likewise thought they should be sold when they grew old and that one should not feed useless slaves. On the whole, he thought nothing superfluous to be a bargain, but that anything that anyone needed, even if sold for a penny, was a good sale. He thought lands should be acquired for sowing and tending rather than for watering and sweeping.

Some people considered these actions to be examples of his meanness, while others approved of this behavior as that of a man who debased himself for the betterment and instruction of others. I reckon it the trait of an overly-obstinate person to cast off and sell one's servants when one has gotten full use out of them as from beasts of burden, believing there is no relation between one human and another beyond that of usefulness. We observe that kindness has a broader field of operation than mere justice. We are born to exercise law and justice solely toward human beings, but we may at times extend acts of kindness and goodwill even to irrational beasts, such acts flowing, one might say, from the abundant spring of human kindness. It is the part of a good man to take care of his horses when they are worn out by old age and of his dogs not just when they are pups but also when they are old.

(*Life of Marcus Cato*, Chapters 4–5)

Suggestions for Further Reading

1. Homer

Lilja, Saara, "Theriophily in Homer."

TEXTS CONSULTED

The translations from Greek and Latin authors included in this anthology employed the editions listed below. For the passages from Philo of Alexandria, see note 3, p. xiii.

Aelian

A.F. Scholfield, ed., *Aelian: On the Characteristics of Animals* (Cambridge, MA: Harvard University Press, 1959).

Alcmaeon and Democritus

Diels, Hermann and Walther Kranz, eds, *Die Fragmente der Vorsokratiker*, 6th edn (Berlin: Weidmann, 1951–52).

Aristotle

Aubonnet, Jean, ed., *Aristote: Politique, Livres I et II* (Paris: Les Belles Lettres, 1968).
——, *Aristote: Politique Livre VII* (Paris: Les Belles Lettres, 1986).
Balme, D.M., and Allan Gotthelf, eds, *Aristotle: Historia Animalium. Volume I: Books I–X: Text* (Cambridge: Cambridge University Press, 2002).
Bywater, I., ed., *Aristotelis Ethica Nicomachea* (Oxford: Clarendon Press, 1894; rept. 1962).
Louis, Pierre, ed., *Aristote: Les Parties des Animaux* (Paris: Les Belles Lettres, 1956).

Augustine

Dombart, B., and A. Kalb, eds, *Sancti Aurelii Augustini de Civitate Dei Libri I-X* (Turnhout: Brepols, 1955 (Corpus Christianorum Series Latina 47).

Chrysippus

von Arnim, Johannes, ed., *Stoicorum Veterum Fragmenta* (Stuttgart: Teubner, 1964; reprint of the edition of 1905).

Cicero

Ax, W., ed., *M. Tulli Ciceronis Scripta Quae Manserunt Omnia, Vol. 45: De Natura Deorum* (Stuttgart: Teubner, 1968).

Moreschini, Claudio, ed., *M. Tullius Cicero Scripta Quae Manserunt Omnia Fasc. 43: De Finibus Bonorum et Malorum* (Munich and Leipzig: Saur, 2005).

L.C. Purser. ed., *M. Tulli Ciceronis Epistulae. Vol. I: Epistulae ad Familiares* (Oxford: Clarendon Press, 1968).

Diogenes Laertius

Long, H.S., *Diogenis Laertii Vitae Philosophorum* (Oxford: Clarendon Press, 1964).

Empedocles

Inwood, Brad., ed., *The Poem of Empedocles: A Text and Translation with Introduction* (Toronto: University of Toronto Press, 2001).

Epicurus

Long, H.S., *Diogenis Laertii Vitae Philosophorum* (Oxford: Clarendon Press, 1964).

Herodotus

Hude, Carolus, ed., *Herodoti Historiae I* (Oxford: Clarendon Press, 1967).

Hesiod

West, M.L., ed., *Hesiod: Works & Days, edited with Prolegomena and Commentary* (Oxford: Clarendon Press, 1978).

Homer

Allen, Thomas W., ed., *Homeri Opera* (Oxford: Clarendon Press, 1966).

Lucretius

Martin, Joseph, ed., *T. Lucreti Cari de Rerum Natura Libri Sex* (Leipzig: Teubner, 1963).

Ovid

Anderson, William S., ed., *P. Ovidii Nasonis Metamorphoses* (Stuttgart and Leipzig: Teubner, 1993).

Plato

Burnet, John, ed., *Platonis Opera* (Oxford: Clarendon Press, 1901–1902; rept. 1962–1967).

Pliny the Elder

Ernout, A., ed., *Pline l'Ancien: Histoire Naturelle, Livre VIII* (Paris: Les Belles Lettres, 1952).

Saint Denis, E. de, ed., *Pline l'Ancien: Histoire Naturelle, Livre IX* (Paris: Les Belles Lettres, 1955).

Plutarch

Casevitz, Michel and Daniel Babut, eds, *Plutarque: Oeuvres Morales XV (Sur les Contradictions Stoïciennes, etc.)* (Paris: Les Belles Lettres, 2004).

Defradas, Jean, Jean Hani and Robert Klaerr, eds, *Plutarque: Oeuvres Morales II* (Paris: Les Belles Lettres, 1985).

Dumortier, Jean and Jean Defradas, eds, *Plutarque: Oeuvres Morales VII: Traités de Morale 27–36* (Paris: Les Belles Lettres, 1975).

Hubert, C., *Plutarchi Moralia, Vol. 6* (Leipzig: Teubner, 1959).

Ziegler, K., ed., *Plutarchus Vitae Parallelae I. 1* (Leipzig: Teubner, 1969).

Porphyry

Bouffartigue, Jean, Michel Patillon, Alain Segond and Luc Brisson, eds, *Porphyre: De l'Abstinence* (Paris: Les Belles Lettres, 1977–1995).

Seneca

Bourgery, A., ed., *Sénèque. Dialogues, Tome Second: De la Vie Heureuse, de la Brièveté de la Vie* (Paris: Les Belles Lettres, 1966).

Reynolds, L.D., *L. Annaei Senecae ad Lucilium Epistulae Morales* (Oxford: Clarendon Press, 1969).

Sextus Empiricus

Mutschmann, Hermannus, ed., *Sexti Empirici Opera* (Leipzig: Teubner, 1912).

Xenophon

Marchant, E.C., ed., *Xenophontis Opera Omnia* (Oxford: Clarendon Press, 1967).

BIBLIOGRAPHY

d'Agostino, Vittorio, "Sulla Zoopsicologia di Plutarco," *Archivo Italiano di Psicologia* 11 (1933) 21–42.

Anderson, J.K., *Hunting in the Ancient World* (Berkeley: University of California Press, 1985).

Armstrong, Susan J. and Richard G. Botzler, eds, *The Animal Ethics Reader* (London: Routledge, 2003).

Bandini, Michele and Federico G. Pericoli, eds, *Scritti in Memoria di Dino Pieraccioni* (Florence: Istituto Papirologico G. Vitelli, 1993).

Barigazzi, Adelmo, "Implicanze Morali nella Polemica Plutarchea sulla Psicologia degli Animali," in Italo Gallo, ed., *Plutarco e le Scienze* (Genoa: Sagep Editrice, 1992) 297–315.

Barringer, Judith M., *The Hunt in Ancient Greece* (Baltimore: Johns Hopkins University Press, 2001).

Bartels, Klaus, *Was Ist der Mensch: Texte zur Anthropologie der Antike* (Munich: Heimeran, 1975).

Beagon, Mary, *Roman Nature: The Thought of Pliny the Elder* (Oxford: Clarendon Press, 1992).

Becchi, Francesco, "Biopsicologia e Giustizia verso gli Animali in Teofrasto e Plutarco," *Prometheus* 27 (2001) 119–135.

——, "Istinto e Intelligenza negli Scritti Zoopsicologici di Plutarco," in Michele Bandini and Federico G. Pericoli, eds, *Scritti in Memoria di Dino Pieraccioni* (Florence: Istituto Papirologico G. Vitelli, 1993).

Boas, George, "Theriophily," in Philip P. Wiener, ed., *Dictionary of the History of Ideas* (New York: Scribners, 1973) IV, 384–389.

Bodson, L., "Aspects of Pliny's Zoology," in Roger French and Frank Greenaway, eds, *Science in the Early Roman Empire: Pliny the Elder, His Sources and Influence* (Totawa, NJ: Barnes and Noble Books, 1986) 98–110.

Boulogne, Jacques, ed., *Les Grecs et les Animaux: Le Cas Remarquable de Plutarque* (Lille: Collection UL3, 2005).

Bréchet, Christophe, "La Philosophie de Gryllos," in Jacques Boulogne, *Les Grecs et les Animaux: Le Cas Remarquable de Plutarque* (Lille: Collection UL3, 2005) 43–61.

Brink, C.O., "Οἰκείωσις and Οἰκειότης: Theophrastus and Zeno on Nature in Moral Theory," *Phronesis* 1 (1955–56) 123–145.

Caballero, Raúl, "ΟΙΚΕΙΩΣΙΣ en Plutarco," in A. Pérez Jiménez, J. García Lopez and R. Ma. Aguilar, eds, *Plutarco, Platón y Aristóteles: Actas del V. Congreso International de la I. P. S. (Madrid-Cuenca, 4–7 de mayo de 1999)* (Madrid: Ediciones Clásicas, 1999) 549–566.

Cartmill, Matt, *A View to a Death in the Morning: Hunting and Nature through History* (Cambridge, MA: Harvard University Press, 1993).

Castignone, Silvana and Giuliana Lanata, eds, *Filosofi e Animali nel Mondo Antico* (Pisa: Edizioni ETS, 1994).

Cassin, Barbara and Jean-Louis Labarrière, eds, *L'Animal dans l'Antiquité* (Paris:Vrin, 1997).

Clark, Gillian, trans., *Porphyry: On Abstinence from Killing Animals* (Ithaca: Cornell University Press, 2000).

Cole, Thomas, *Democritus and the Sources of Greek Anthropology* (Cleveland: Press of Western Reserve University, 1967).

DeLacy, Philip, "The Epicurean Analysis of Language," *AJPh* 60 (1939) 85–92.

Devereux, Daniel and Pierre Pellegrin, eds, *Biologie, Logique et Métaphysique chez Aristote* (Paris: Éditions du Centre Nationale de la Recherche Scientifique, 1990).

Dickerman, Sherwood Owen, "Some Stock Illustrations of Animal Intelligence in Greek Psychology," *TAPhA* 42 (1911) 123–130.

Dierauer, Urs, "Raison ou Instinct? Le Développement de la Zoopsychologie Antique," in Barbara Cassin and Jean-Louis Labarrière, eds, *L'Animal dans l'Antiquité* (Paris: Vrin, 1997) 3–29.

——, *Tier und Mensch im Denken der Antike: Studien zur Tierpsychologie, Anthropologie und Ethik* (Amsterdam: Grüner, 1977).

——, "Das Verhältnis von Mensch und Tier im griechisch-römischen Denken," in Paul Münch and Rainer Walz, eds, *Tiere und Menschen: Geschichte und Aktualität eines prekären Verhältnisses* (Paderborn: Schöningh, 1998) 37–85.

Dirlmeier, Franz, "Die Oikeiosis-Lehre Theophrasts," *Philologus Supplementband* (1937) 1–100.

Dombrowski, Daniel A., *The Philosophy of Vegetarianism* (Amherst: University of Massachusetts Press, 1984).

——, "Vegetarianism and the Argument from Marginal Cases in Porphyry," *JHI* 45 (1984) 141–143.

Dumont, Jacques, *Les Animaux dans l'Antiquité* (Paris: l'Harmattan, 2001).

Fernández Delgado, José Antonio and Francesca Pordomingo Pardo, eds, *Estudios sobre Plutarco: Aspectos Formales* (Salamanca: Ediciones Clásicas, 1996).

Fögen, Thorsten, "Animals in Graeco-Roman Antiquity and Beyond," www.telemachos.hu-berlin.de/esterni/Tierbibliographie_Foegen.pdf.

Fortenbaugh, William W., "Aristotle: Animals, Emotion and Moral Virtue," *Arethusa* 4 (1972) 137–165.

—— and Robert W. Sharples, eds, *Theophrastean Studies on Natural Science, Physics and Metaphysics, Ethics, Religion, and Rhetoric* (New Brunswick: Transaction Books, 1988).

French, Roger, *Ancient Natural History: Histories of Nature* (London and New York: Routledge, 1994).

—— and Frank Greenaway, eds, *Science in the Early Roman Empire: Pliny the Elder, His Sources and Influence* (Totawa, NJ: Barnes and Noble Books, 1986).

Frère, Jean, *La Bestiaire de Platon* (Paris: Éditions Kimé, 1998).

Gallo, Italo, ed., *Plutarco e le Scienze* (Genoa: Sagep Editrice, 1992).

Gautier, David P., *Morals by Agreement* (Oxford: Clarendon Press, 1986).

Gilhus, Ingvild, *Animals, Gods and Humans: Changing Attitudes to Animals in Greek, Roman and Early Christian Ideas* (Oxford: Routledge, 2006).

Gill, James E., "Theriophily in Antiquity: A Supplementary Account," *JHI* 30 (1969) 401–412.

Hauser, Marc D., *Wild Minds: What Animals Really Think* (New York: Henry Holt, 2000).

Haussleiter, Johannes, *Der Vegetarismus in der Antike* (Berlin: Töpelmann, 1935).

Heath, John, *The Talking Greeks: Speech, Animals and the Other in Homer, Aeschylus, and Plato* (Cambridge: Cambridge University Press, 2005).

Huby, Pamela M., "The Epicureans, Animals, and Freewill," *Apeiron* 3 (1969) 17–19.

Hughes, J. Donald, *Ecology in Ancient Civilizations* (Albuquerque: University of New Mexico Press, 1975).

——, "Hunting in the Ancient Mediterranean World," in Linda Kalof, ed., *A Cultural History of Animals in Antiquity* (Oxford: Berg, 2007) 47–70.

Jufresa, Montserrat, "La Abstinencia de Carne y el Origen de la Civilización," in José Antonio Fernández Delgado and Francesca Pordomingo Pardo, eds, *Estudios sobre Plutarco: Pectos Formales* (Salamanca: Ediciones Clásicas, 1996) 219–226.

Kalof, Linda, ed., *A Cultural History of Animals in Antiquity* (Oxford: Berg, 2007).

—— and Amy Fitzgerald, eds, *The Animals Reader* (Oxford: Berg-Palgrave, 2007).

Kitts, David B., "Plato on Kinds of Animals," *Biology and Philosophy* 2 (1987) 315–328.

Körner, Otto, *Die Homerische Tierwelt* (Munich: Bergmann, 1930).

Labarrière, Jean-Louis, "De la Phronesis Animale," in Daniel Devereux and Pierre Pellegrin, eds, *Biologie, Logique et Métaphysique clez Aristote* (Paris: Éditions du Centre National de la Recherche Scientifique, 1990) 405–428.

Lilja, Saara, "Theriophily in Homer," *Arctos* 8 (1974) 71–78.

Long, A.A., ed., *Problems in Stoicism* (London: Athlone Press, 1971).

Lorenz, Günter, *Tiere im Leben der alten Kulturen: Schriftlose Kulture, Alter Orient, Ägypten, Griechenland und Rom* (Vienna: Böhlau, 2000).

Lovejoy, Arthur O. and George Boas, *Primitivism and Related Ideas in Antiquity* (Baltimore: Johns Hopkins University Press, 1935).

Martin, Hubert, "Plutarch's *De Sollertia Animalium* 959B-C: The Discussion of the Encomium on Hunting," *AJPh* 100 (1979) 99–106.

Martos Montiel, Juan Francisco, "*Sophrosyne* o *Akrasía*: Los Animales como Modelo de Comportamiento en los *Moralia* de Plutarco," in José Antonio Fernández Delgado and Francisca Pordomingo Pardo, eds, *Estudios sobre Plutarco: Aspectos Formales* (Salamanca: Ediciones Clásicas, 1996) 205–210.

Mitsis, Phillip, *Epicurus' Ethical Theory: The Pleasures of Invulnerability* (Ithaca: Cornell, 1988).

Mühl, Max, "Der λόγος ἐνδιάθετος und προφορικός von der älteren Stoa bis zur Synode von Sirmium 351," *Archiv für Begriffsgeschichte* 7 (1962) 7–56.

Münch, Paul and Rainer Walz, eds, *Tiere und Menschen: Geschichte und Aktualität eines prekären Verhältnisses* (Paderborn: Schöningh, 1998).

Newmyer, Stephen T., "Animal *Philanthropia* in the *Convivium Septem Sapientium*," in José Ribiero, Delfim Leão, Manuel Tröster and Paula Barata Dias, eds, *Symposion and Philanthropia in Plutarch* (Coimbra: Centro de Estudos Clássicas e Humanisticos da Universidade de Coimbra, 2009) 497–504.

——, *Animals, Rights and Reason in Plutarch and Modern Ethics* (Oxford: Routledge, 2006).

——, "Calculating Creatures: Ancients and Moderns on Understanding of Number in Animals," *QUCC* 89, 2 (2008) 117–124.

——, "The Human Soul and the Animal Soul: Stoic Theory and Its Survival in Contractualist Ethics," in Annetta Alexandridis, Markus Wild and Lorenz Winkler-Horaček, eds, *Mensch und Tier in der Antike: Grenzziehung und Grenzüberschreitung* (Wiesbaden: Reichert Verlag, 2008) 71–80.

——, "Ovid on the Moral Grounds for Vegetarianism," in Werner Schubert, ed., *Ovid: Werk und Wirkung: Festgabe für Michael von Albrecht zum 65. Geburtstag*, I (Frankfurt: Peter Lang, 1998) 477–486.

——, "Paws to Reflect: Ancients and Moderns on the Religious Sensibilities of Animals," *QUCC* 75, 3 (2003) 111–129.

——, "Philo on Animal Psychology: Sources and Moral Implications," in Samuel Kottek and Manfred Horstmanshoff, eds, *From Athens to Jerusalem: Medicine in Ancient Jewish and Early Christian Literature* (Rotterdam: Erasmus Publishing, 2000) 143–155.

——, "Plutarch on Justice toward Animals: Ancient Insights on a Modern Debate," *Scholia: Natal Studies in Classical Antiquity* 1 (1992) 38–54.

——, "Plutarch on the Moral Grounds for Vegetarianism," *CO* 72 (1995) 41–43.

——, "Speaking of Beasts: the Stoics and Plutarch on Animal Reason and the Modern Case against Animals," *QUCC* 63, 3 (1999) 99–110.

Nicolay, Eveline, "Homère et l'Âme des Bêtes," in Friedrich Niewöhner and Jean-Loup Sebon, eds, *Die Seele der Tiere* (Wiesbaden: Harassowitz Verlag, 2001) 51–58.

Niewöhner, Friedrich and Jean-Loup Sebon, eds, *Die Seele der Tiere* (Wiesbaden: Harassowitz Verlag, 2001).

Obbink, Dirk, "The Origins of Greek Sacrifice: Theophrastus on Religion and Cultural History," in William W. Fortenbaugh and Robert Sharples, eds, *Theophrastean Studies on Natural Science, Physics and Metaphysics, Ethics, Religion, and Rhetoric* (New Brunswick: Transaction Books, 1988) 272–295.

Pembroke, S.J., "Oikeiôsis," in A.A. Long, ed., *Problems in Stoicism* (London: Athlone, 1971) 114–149.

Pérez-Jiménez, A., J. García Lopez and R. Ma. Aguilar, eds, *Plutarco, Platón y Aristóteles. Actas del V. Congreso Internacional de la I. P. S. (Madria-Cuenca, 4–7 de Mayo de 1999* (Madrid: Ediciones Clásicas, 1999).

Pérez-Paoli, Ubaldo, "Porphyrios' Gedanken zur Gerechtigkeit gegenüber den Tieren," in Friedrich Niewöhner and Jean-Loup Sebon, eds, *Die Seele der Tiere* (Wiesbaden: Harassowitz Verlag, 2001) 93–110.

Pinotti, Patrizia, "Gli Animali in Platone: Metafore e Tassonomie," in Silvana Castignone and Giuliana Lanata, eds, *Filosofi e Animali nel Mondo Antico* (Pisa: Edizioni ETS, 1994) 101–121.

Pratt, Vernon, "The Essence of Aristotle's Zoology," *Phronesis* 29 (1984) 267–278.

Preus, Anthony, "Animal and Human Souls in the Peripatetic School," *Skepsis* 1 (1990) 67–99.

——, "Biological Theory in Porphyry's *De abstinentia*," *Ancient Philosophy* 3 (1983) 149–159.

——, *Science and Philosophy in Aristotle's Biological Works* (Hildesheim: Olms, 1975).

Rahn, Helmut, "Das Tier in der homerischen Dichtung," *Studium Generale* 20 (1967) 90–105.

——, "Tier und Mensch in der homerischen Auffassung der Wirklichkeit," *Paideuma* 5 (1953) 277–297 and 431–480.

Regan, Tom and Peter Singer, eds, *Animal Rights and Human Obligations* (Englewood Cliffs, NJ: Prentice Hall, 1976).

Renehan, Robert, "The Greek Anthropocentric View of Man," *HSCPh* 85 (1981) 239–259.

Reydams-Schils, Gretchen, "Human Bonding and *Oikeiōsis* in Roman Stoicism," *OSAPh* 22 (2002) 221–251.

Ribiero, José, Delfim Leão, Manuel Tröster and Paula Barata Dias, eds, *Symposion and Philanthropia in Plutarch* (Coimbra: Centro de Estudos Clássicas e Humanisticos da Universidade de Coimbra, 2009).

Rundin, John, "The Vegetarianism of Empedocles in Its Historical Context," *The Ancient World* 29 (1998) 19–35.

Ryder, Richard D., *Animal Revolution: Changing Attitudes towards Speciesism* (Oxford: Blackwell, 1989).

Santese, Giuseppina, "Animali e Razionalità in Plutarco," in Silvana Castignone and Giuliana Lanata, eds, *Filosofi e Animali nel Mondo Antico* (Pisa: Edizioni ETS, 1994).

Schubert, Werner, ed., *Ovid: Werk und Wirkung: Festgabe für Michael von Albrecht zum 65. Geburtstag*, I (Frankfurt: Peter Lang, 1998).

Shelton, Jo-Ann, "Beastly Spectacles in the Ancient Mediterranean World," in Linda Kalof, ed., *A Cultural History of Animals in Antiquity* (Oxford: Berg, 2007) 97–126.

——, "Contracts with Animals: Lucretius, *De Rerum Natura*," *Between the Species* 11 (1995) 115–121.

——, "Lucretius and the Use and Abuse of Animals," *Eranos* 94 (1996) 48–64.

Singer, Peter, *Animal Liberation: A New Ethic for Our Treatment of Animals* (New York: Avon, 1975).

Solmsen, Friedrich, "Antecedents of Aristotle's Psychology and Scale of Beings," *AJPh* 76 (1955) 148–164.

Sorabji, Richard, *Animal Minds and Human Morals: The Origins of the Western Debate* (Ithaca: Cornell University Press, 1993).

Steiner, Gary, *Animals and the Moral Community: Mental Life, Moral Status, and Kinship* (New York: Columbia University Press, 2008).

——, *Anthropocentrism and Its Discontents* (Pittsburgh: University of Pittsburgh Press, 2005).

Striker, Gisela, "The Role of *Oikeiosis* in Stoic Ethics," *OSAPh* 1 (1983) 145–167.

Tabarroni, Andrea, "On Articulation and Animal Language in Ancient Linguistic Theory," *Versus* 50–51 (1988) 103–121.

Terian, Abraham, "A Critical Introduction to Philo's Dialogues," *ANRW* II. 21, 1 (1984) 272–294.

——, *Philonis Alexandrini de Animalibus: The Armenian Text with an Introduction, Translation and Commentary* (Chico, CA: Scholars Press, 1981).

Tovar Paz, Francisco-Javier, "El Motivo de la 'Caza' in *De Sollertia Animalium* de Plutarco," in José Antonio Fernández and Francisca Pordomingo Pardo, eds, *Estudios sobre Plutarco: Aspectos Formales* (Salamanca: Ediciones Clásicas, 1996) 211–217.

Tsekourakis, Damianos, "Pythagoreanism or Platonism and Ancient Medicine? The Reasons for Vegetarianism in Plutarch's Moralia," *ANRW* II. 36, 1 (1987) 366–393.

van der Stockt, Luc, "Plutarch and Dolphins: Love Is All You Need," in Jacques Boulogne, ed., *Les Grecs et les Animaux: Le Cas Remarquable de Plutarque* (Lille: Collection UL3, 2005) 43–61.

Vegetti, Mario, "Figure dell' Animale in Aristotele," in Silvana Castignone and Giuliana Lanata, eds, *Filosofi e Animale nel Mondo Antico* (Pisa: Edizioni ETS, 1994) 123–137.

deWaal, Frans, *The Age of Empathy: Nature's Lessons for a Kinder Society* (New York: Harmony Books, 2009).

——, *Good Natured: The Origins of Right and Wrong in Humans and Other Animals* (Cambridge, MA: Harvard University Press, 1996).

Wiener, Philip P., ed., *Dictionary of the History of Ideas* (New York: Scribners, 1973).

PASSAGES DISCUSSED

Passages indicated in **boldface** are translated in the anthology, on the page noted in **boldface**.

DK = Hermann Diels and Walther Kranz, eds, *Die Fragmente der Vorsokratiker*, 6th edn (Berlin: Weidmann, 1951–52)
SVF = Johannes von Arnim, ed., *Stoicorum Veterum Fragmenta* (Stuttgart: Teubner, 1964; reprint of the edition of 1905).

Aelian

On the Nature of Animals (**Prologue**) **39**; (III. 23) 84; (**VI. 50**) **19**; (VII. 1) 57; (VII. 4) 54; (VII. 7) 85

Alcmaeon

(**fr. 1a DK**) 3

Aristotle

History of Animals (**488a20–26**) **9**; (**588a16–18–588b3**) **9–10**; (588a24) 7; (**588b4–12**) **9**; (615b23–24) 84; *Metaphysics* (**980a28–981a4**) **10**; *Nicomachean Ethics* (**1161a30–1162b2**) **74–75**, 8; (**1097b33–1098a4**) **10**; *On Interpretation* (16a28–29) 61; *On the Soul* (414a19) 8; *Parts of Animals* (644b22–645a23) 7; (646a10–12) 7; (**660a35–660b2**) **61**; (**681a10–15**) **9**; (686a27) 12; (687a19–23) 8; *Politics* (**1253a9–18**) **75**; (1253a10–11) 61; (1253a11–14) 61; (**1256b15–23**) **27**; (1256b15–26) 8; (1256b23–26) 78; (1280b37) 89; (**1332b3–8**) **10**; *Rhetoric* (1373b14–16) 100; *Topica* (142b23–28) 57

Augustine

City of God (**I. 20**) **22–23**; *Confessions* (VII. 17) 21

Chrysippus

(*SVF* 2. 821) **4**

Cicero

Laws (I. 8. 24) 31; *Letters to Atticus* (XII. 52. 3) 41; *Letters to His Friends* (**VII. 1. 3**) **94**; *On Duties* (**I. 50**) **84**; *On the Ends of Good and Evil* (**II. 109–110**) **41–42**; (**III. 67**) **77**; *On the Nature of the Gods* (**II. 154–159**) **76–77**; *Tusculan Disputations* (I. 39) 101

Democritus

(**DK 257–258**) **83–84**

Diogenes Laertius

Lives of the Philosophers (VI. 25–26) 101; (**VII. 55**) **60**; (**VII. 85**) **28**; (VII. 85–86) 45; (VII. 127) 66; (**VII. 129**) **74**, 76, 78; (**VIII. 13**) **98**; (VIII. 20) 90; (**VIII. 36**) **114**; (VIII. 53) 100; (VIII. 77) 100; (IX. 79) 64; (**X. 150** = Epicurus, *Sovereign Maxims* **31–32**) **29**

Empedocles

(**fr. 11 and 124 Inwood = DK 115 and 139**) **101**

Epicurus

Sovereign Maxims (**31–32**) **29**

Herodotus

Histories (**I. 23–24**) **50–51**

Hesiod

Works and Days (109–126) 102; (**274–280**) **83**; (**277–280**) **19**, 78

Homer

Iliad (**IX. 314–327**) **40**; *Odyssey* (**XVII. 290–323**) **113–114**, 40; (XVII. 326–327) 113

Lucretius

On the Nature of Things (**V. 855–877**) **30**

Ovid

Metamorphoses (I. 89–112) 102; (**XV 75–142**) 97, **99–100**; (XV. 143–478) 98

Philo of Alexandria

On Animals (10–71) 11; (12) 61; (**11–12**) **13**; (**17**) **13**; (**29**) **13**; (30–65) 55; (38) 57; (**44**) **45**; (**45**) **14**; (**61**) **85**; (**64**) **85;** (**66**) **56**; (66–70) 55; (**68**) **56**; (**70**) **56**; (**71**) **14**; (**77–78**) **57**; (77–100) 11, 55; (**85**) **14**; (**96**) **85–86**; (**98**) **62**; (**100**) **30**

Plato

Laws (766a) 4; (**781e–783b**) **103**; (823d) 87; (**824b–c**) 87, **88**; (961d) 5; *Phaedo* (81e–82b) 5; (114d) 5; *Phaedrus* (249b) 5; *Protagoras* (320c–322d) 54; (322a) 31; *Republic* (**372 a–d**) **102**; (427–445e) 55; (**440e–441b**) **6**; (563c) 4; (620d) 5; *Symposium* (**207a–c**) **5–6**; *Timaeus* (42c) 5; (91e–92a) 12, 54

Pliny the Elder

Natural History (**VIII. 1**) **31**, 54; (VIII. 20–21) 93; (IX. 24) 49; (**IX. 24–25**) **51**; (**IX. 28**) **51**; (**IX. 33**) **51**

Plutarch

Banquet of the Seven Sages (**160E–161E**) **52**; (161D) 50; *Life of Marcus Cato* (**Chapters 4 and 5**) **115**; *On the Cleverness of Animals* (959A–965D) 17; (**959B–E**) **88–89**; (959E–963F) 80; (**959F**) 97; (960A) 66, 77; (**960A–B**) **17–18**; (**960C**) **18**; (**960D–E**) **18**; (960E–F = Porphyry, *On Abstinence from Animal Flesh* III. 21. 5–7) 47; (**961B**) 46; (**962A**) **58**, 80; (**962A–B**) **43**; (962C) 57; (962E) 85; (963A) 57; (**963F–965B**) **78–80**; (964A) 108; (964B) 82; (972B) 48, 54; (**972F–973E**) **63**; (**974 A–B, D–E**) **58**; (975A) 85; (**975E–F**) **32–33**; *On the Eating of Flesh* (993A) 106; (**993C–994B**) **106–107**; (**994E**) **63–64**; (994F) 106; (**995D–996A**) **107–108**; (995E) 106; (**996E–997A**) **108**; (998D) 106; *On the Love of Offspring* (**493B–D**) **43**; (**495A–B**) **43**; *On the Self-Contradictions of the Stoics* (**1038B**) **33**; *Precepts for Preserving Health* (**131F–132A**) **106**; *Whether Beasts Are Rational* (**987B–F**) **37–38**; (990D) 54; (**991F**) **18**; (**992B–D**) **18–19**

Porphyry

On Abstinence from Animals Flesh (**I. 4**) **109**; (**II. 7**) 109; (**II. 12, 34**) **90–91**; (**II. 13**) **109–110**; (II. 33–61) 20; (**III. 2–4**) **66–68**; (III. 3) 21; (III. 3. 4) 20; (III. 3. 20–III. 24. 5) 20, 80; (III. 5) 90; (III. 5–32) 90; (**III. 6. 5–6**) **21**; (III. 7. 1) 20; (**III. 7. 2**) **21**; (**III. 11–12, 18**) **81**; (**III. 13. 1–3**) **33–34**; (III. 20) 74, 75; (**III. 21. 5–7** = Plutarch, *On the Cleverness of Animals* **960E-F**) **47**

Seneca

Moral Letters (**7. 2–4**) **94–95**; (**76. 8–10**) **15**; (108. 13–16) 104; (**108. 17–23**) **104–105**; (**121. 7–13**) **45–46**; *On the Shortness of Life* (**13. 6–7**) **95**

Sextus Empiricus

Outlines of Pyrrhonism (**I. 62–67, 72–76**) 64–65

Suetonius

Titus (17) 93

Xenophon

Memorabilia (*Recollections of Socrates*) (I. 4. 13) 12, 31; (**I. 4. 11–14**) 54

Related titles from Routledge

Animals, Gods and Humans
Changing attitudes to animals in Greek, Roman and Early Christian thought
Ingvild Sælid Gilhus

Ingvild Sælid Gilhus explores the transition from traditional Greek and Roman religion to Christianity in the Roman Empire and the effect of this change on the concept of animals, illustrating the main factors in the creation of a Christian conception of animals. One of the underlying assumptions of the book is that changes in the way animal motifs are used and the way human–animal relations are conceptualized serve as indicators of more general cultural shifts. Gilhus attests that in late antiquity, animals were used as symbols in a general redefinition of cultural values and assumptions.

A wide range of key texts are consulted and range from philosophical treaties to novels and poems on metamorphoses; from biographies of holy persons such as Apollonius of Tyana and Antony, the Christian desert ascetic, to natural history; from the New Testament via Gnostic texts to the church fathers; from pagan and Christian criticism of animal sacrifice to the acts of the martyrs. Both the pagan and the Christian conception of animals remained rich and multilayered through the centuries and this book presents the dominant themes and developments in the conception of animals without losing that complexity.

ISBN: 978–0–415–38649–4 (hbk)
ISBN: 978–0–415–38650–0 (pbk)

Available at all good bookshops
For ordering and further information please visit:
www.routledge.com

Related titles from Routledge

Animals, Rights and Reason in Plutarch and Modern Ethics

Stephen T. Newmyer

Plutarch is virtually unique in surviving classical authors in arguing that animals are rational and sentient and in concluding that human beings must take notice of their interests. Stephen Newmyer explores Plutarch's three animal-related treatises, as well as passages from his other ethical treatises, which argue that non-human animals are rational and therefore deserve to fall within the sphere of human moral concern. Newmyer shows that some of the arguments Plutarch raises strikingly foreshadow those found in the works of such prominent animal rights philosophers as Peter Singer and Tom Regan in maintaining that non-human animals are the sorts of creatures that have intellectual qualities that cause them to be proper objects of man's concern, and have interests and desires that entitle them to respect from their human counterparts. This volume is groundbreaking in viewing Plutarch's views not only in the context of ancient philosophical and ethical thought, but in its place, generally overlooked, in the history of speculation on human–animal relations, and in pointing out how remarkably Plutarch differs from such predominantly anti-animal thinkers as the Stoics.

ISBN: 978–0–415–24046–8 (hbk)
ISBN: 978–0–415–24047–5 (pbk)

Available at all good bookshops
For ordering and further information please visit:
www.routledge.com

Ancient Ethics

Susan Sauvé Meyer

To understand ethical theory we need to understand its origins, just as knowledge of ancient philosophy cannot be complete without an understanding of the ethical tradition which formed such a crucial part of it. *Ancient Ethics* is a clear and thorough introduction to the birth of ethics in ancient Greece and Rome for anyone starting out in ethics.

Here Susan Sauvé Meyer details a history of ethical thought, from its beginnings in the writings of Plato and Aristotle through its development in the Hellenistic period by Epicureans and Stoics, with lucid and accessible explanations of their theories.

Throughout, she critically assesses the arguments on which their thoughts were based, incorporating the responses of their contemporary critics as well as modern-day assessments to show the reader how to think and critique philosophically.

This book will be ideal for anyone beginning an introductory course in ancient ethics or moral theory, anyone interested in learning more about the history of ethical philosophy, or simply those who wish to learn "how to live well".

ISBN: 978–0–415–94026–9 (hbk)
ISBN: 978–0–415–94027–6 (pbk)
ISBN: 978–0–203–64389–1 (ebk)

Related titles from Routledge

The Encyclopedia of Ancient Natural Scientists
The Greek tradition and its many heirs
Edited by Paul T. Keyser and Georgia Irby-Massie

The Encyclopedia of Ancient Natural Scientists is the first comprehensive English language work to provide a survey of all ancient natural science, from its beginnings through the end of Late Antiquity. A team of over 100 of the world's experts in the field have compiled this *Encyclopedia*, including entries which are not mentioned in any other reference work – resulting in a unique and hugely ambitious resource which will prove indispensable for anyone seeking the details of the history of ancient science.

Additional features include a Glossary, Gazetteer, and Time-Line. The Glossary explains many Greek (or Latin) terms difficult to translate, whilst the Gazetteer describes the many locales from which scientists came. The Time-Line shows the rapid rise in the practice of science in the fifth century BCE and rapid decline after Hadrian, due to the centralization of Roman power, with consequent loss of a context within which science could flourish.

ISBN: 978–0–415–34020–5 (hbk)

Related titles from Routledge

The Animal Ethics Reader
Second Edition
Edited by Susan Armstrong and Richard G. Botzler

"This ambitious anthology is a welcome resource for the study of the ethical issues of human interactions with other animals. The editors have provided a volume that covers a wide and diverse range of topics and points of view."

Anthrozoos, 18 (4) 2005.

The second edition of *The Animal Ethics Reader* is the most current and comprehensive anthology of readings on the subject of animal ethics. Whilst keeping the best of the previous edition, the editors have updated readings to reflect ongoing developments and emerging issues like rehabilitation of oiled wildlife, human–elephant interactions, and animal consciousness and emotion.

Classic and contemporary readings are arranged thematically, carefully presenting a balanced representation of the field as it stands, and include selections from leading experts in the field. Each chapter is introduced by the editors and study questions feature at the end.

The second edition also contains a new foreword by Bernard Rollin.

ISBN: 978–0–415–94027–6 (pbk)